SCENES FROM THE PAST:
THE RAILWAYS AR
GRIMSBY
CLEETHORPES, IMMINGHAM
& North-East Lincolnshire

Grimsby Town, 30th September 1959. The Class B1 4-6-0 about to pass the signal box is leaving platform 1 and is signalled to take the left hand fork at Garden Street with a train for Cleethorpes. Looking on from platform 2, another B1, No. 61284 will shortly leave with a Peterborough train, taking the right hand fork at the junction.
Photo: J. H. Price

COMPILED and WRITTEN by

PAUL KING & DAVE HEWINS

Copyright © P . King , D . R . Hewins, Foxline Publishing

ISBN 1 870119 04 5   Reprinted 1989, 1998.

Designed and edited by Gregory K. Fox

Printed by The Amadeus Press Ltd., Huddersfield

Published by Foxline Publishing
32 Urwick Road, Romiley, Stockport

Acknowledgements

Some time ago two novice authors decided it was time that a book was published on the railways of the Grimsby area. Great dreams were soon shattered as we apparently realised how little material was readily available. Gradually though, through advertisements in shops and the local press, and by talking with other local enthusiasts, information and photographs became available. Without such material, this book would not have been possible, so eventually and with sufficient information to hand, the project was started some two years ago.

We are now in a position to say thank you to those people who made it possible. The list is long and there may be ommissions but to the following and to those we have missed, may we say *THANK YOU*. Eric Green, Mrs. Joan Baker, David Stockton, Ken Pudsey. Noel Camplejohn, Roger Ellis, Ron Dane, Chris Payne, John Willerton, David Lee, John Hewson, John McCulloch, Chris Birchmore (on behalf of the Grimsby-Louth RPS), J. H. Price, Neville Stead, Gordon Biddle, Douglas Thompson, John Meredith, David Packer (for permission to use the late Jack Gready views), Roy Barnard, John Edgington, H. B. Priestley, Brian Miller, R. H. G. Simpson, Pat Loftis, J. R. Morten, G. Coltas, Mick Hales, H. C. Casserley, Lens of Sutton, George Black of the Grimsby Evening Telegraph, Grimsby Public Libraries, Welholme Galleries, Immingham Museum, numerous members of British Railways past and present, David Jackson, Brian Longbone and Roger Milnes of the Great Central Railway Society and Barry Herbert and Alf Ludlam whose Louth Bardney book (Oakwood Press) could well be said to be the spark that kindled the flame. We would also like to take this opportunity to apologise to Brian Clark of York as we inadvertently credited four of his photographs to Grimsby Public Libraries in the 1st edition of this book.

Our special thanks are extended to Greg Fox who has had the courage to add our work to his excellent series of *Scenes From The Past*. Finally to Jane and Liz, our wives, who have stood by us through long hours when they must have felt like railway widows. Our thanks are due to them for without their support we would have foundered within weeks of starting.

Finally, an appeal. We would like to consider a companion volume to this one but desperately need your help and if you have any photographs or information relating to this area, in particular regarding goods traffic, industrial operations and the railway owned shipping fleet, please contact either of us. Our numbers are in the phone book, or call in at the model shop at 7 East St. Marys Gate, Grimsby.

Paul King
Dave Hewins
Grimsby, Sept 1988

Cleethorpes. The visiting locomotive crews of excursions arriving at Cleethorpes were relieved by local men at the platform who then shunted the stock out of the platform before servicing the locomotive. This included watering and turning before returning to pick up its carriages and stabling the whole ensemble for the day at either New Clee or Suggitts Lane. An easy task one might think, but it was not an instance of one relief crew per train for after stabling one the crew returned for another then another until the whole lot were safely stored. The locomotives had to be tended throughout the day, so as evening approached it was necessary to return all the excursions to the station, in the right order, before signing off and going home for a well earned rest. After arrival at platform 5 with an excursion, Class D11 4-4-0 No. 62669 *Ypres*, is taken over by the relief crew, the fireman busily engaged in pulling coal forward.

Photo: N. E. Stead

Introduction

On the 1st of March 1848, one hundred and forty years ago, the first public railway service in the Grimsby area, that between Louth on the East Lincolnshire Railway, and New Holland on the Manchester, Sheffield and Lincolnshire Railway, began. The coming of the railway, which for the first few months had no physical connection with the rest of Britain's railway network, breathed new life into a sterile area of the country. Grimsby and the surrounding area was about to experience its own version of the industrial revolution.

The area covered in this book is, to most devotees, a railway desert somewhere to the east of Doncaster. It was off the beaten track and did not witness the glamourous trains that were on view along the ECML. It is our intention therefore, in the following pages, to illustrate what was missed and hopefully disprove the theory that cameras were banned from taking railway photographs north of Louth and east of Doncaster and Lincoln. The photographs covering Grimsby alone were selected from a vast collection and many more exist but were not available for use for one reason or another. The task, as indeed it proved to be of selecting the final views shown, took many hours and caused much heart searching as personal favourites were rejected. Why leave them out if they were favourites? Unfortunately we fell into the all too familiar trap of choosing excellent views of locomotives which, unless one knows the area well, could have been taken almost anywhere, whereas we were originally rejecting the type of photograph that was needed to show the railway scene in the area. Our first meeting with Greg Fox showed us the error of our ways and for this we owe him our sincere thanks to enable us to produce a book which revives, nostalgically, the railways in an area and not the locomotives passing through it.

It is also hoped to disprove the assumption that any goods traffic emanating from Grimsby consisted entirely of fish trains. The commercial docks imported many different types of product, especially timber from Scandinavia and dairy products from Denmark, all of which originally left the town by rail. Incoming goods traffic consisted mainly of coal and steel, but in recent years, petroleum, oil and chemical products have also used the rail network, tipping the balance to a large extent from traditional traffic. There were also the iron ore trains from High Dyke (Grantham) to the steelworks at Scunthorpe which, from the 1950's, were routed over the East Lincolnshire line through Louth and Grimsby.

Similarly, the majority of visitors arriving in the area came on summer excursions and were not aware of the fairly intensive passenger services being operated. As well as the services starting and terminating in the area such as Cleethorpes to New Holland or Immingham, Grimsby to Louth or New Holland to Barton or Immingham, trains left Cleethorpes and Grimsby for a variety of destinations such as Peterborough, London (Kings Cross), Lincoln, Leicester, Nottingham, Birmingham, Sheffield, Doncaster, Manchester, Liverpool, Leeds and Bournemouth, this latter town via the much lamented Somerset and Dorset route. Though not a complete list, it does show the extent of passenger services that the area has seen at different times throughout the years.

Finally, there are the Grimsby – Immingham trams, not at first glance a railway subject, but an undertaking that always belonged to the railways, having been built by the GCR before passing to the LNER at the grouping in 1923 and finally to British Railways on nationalisation in 1948.

All in all the railway scene in and around Grimsby was always varied and interesting, and it is hoped that in the following pages the reader will share that interest recalled by our efforts.

PLEASE RETAIN THIS BILL FOR REFERENCE   AT57/R

SEASIDE EXCURSION
to
CLEETHORPES
THURSDAY 4th JUNE, 1953

ROAD AND RAIL

BRITISH RAILWAYS
and
MIDLAND GENERAL OMNIBUS CO. LTD.

1. Cleethorpes, c.1931. A sight so familiar on a late Sunday afternoon at Suggitts Lane, Cleethorpes. Tired day trippers will be making their weary way back to Cleethorpes station to board their carriages for the journey home to Yorkshire and the North Midlands and the crews of the excursions are beginning to prepare their locos for the homeward journey. The blowers are on on two Class J39 0-6-0's, a Robinson GCR Director Class 11E (LNER D10) 4-4-0 and 6087 a member of probably the most graceful class of locomotive owned by the GCR an 8B (LNER C4) 4-4-2, otherwise known as Jersey Lilies, as they are prepared on a sunny summers evening in 1931.

Photo: N. Camplejohn

2. Grimsby Town, c.1952. Grimsby Town station from the air circa 1952. A Class J94 0-6-0ST on pilot duty is alongside the cattle dock with a rake of coaches from platform 2 whilst at the other end of the platform a B1 4-6-0 awaits departure with the rest of the train. A short goods, hauled by a Class O2 2-8-0, is standing in the up loop whilst parcels vans are ready for loading in the bay at the far end of platform 1. Coal wagons can be seen in the siding alongside Wellowgate but note that there is no footbridge at this point, not having been built until 1954. At the top of the photograph, Garden Street signal box stands guard over the junction with the East Lincs line curving away to the right. Overlooking the station is the Yarborough Hotel which has hopefully now found a new lease of life after several years of closure when demolition was a distinct possibility. On the opposite side of Bethlehem Street from the hotel is Easons Travel Agency, an organization whose exploits with the famous "Easons Specials" to London during the 1920's and 30's are almost legendary.

Modernisation and rationalisation in recent years has markedly changed the railway scene. The station now has a new roof and the bay at the end of platform 1 has become a car park. The loop lines have been lifted and the cattle dock is derelict and the East Lincs no longer branches off at Garden Street. The level crossing gates at Wellowgate have been replaced by lifting barriers although a bell still rings whenever the crossings close to allow a train into platform 1. *Photo: E. Green*

Railways around Grimsby: 1 : Genesis 1844-1899

The railways of today are but a shadow of their former selves, but in their time they have laid their permanent way across sparsley populated tracts of land, leaving behind them the genesis of thriving new towns.

Grimsby, Immingham and Cleethorpes are all well known in their own rights, with the former as the one time premier fishing port in the world, Immingham for its commercial docks and Cleethorpes as a seaside resort. The south bank of the Humber from Grimsby through to Killingholme is also well known for its chemical and oil related industries. How many people living along the south bank though realise that without the coming of the railways, in particular the Manchester, Sheffield & Lincolnshire, it is unlikely that any of these towns would have developed in the way they have? To start with, Grimsby would possibly be still nothing more than a large village with the remains of an ancient silted up dock as a pointer to its potential. Immingham almost certainly would never have developed into the small town it is today, whilst Cleethorpes, which before the coming of the railway consisted of little more than a few fishermans shacks, may well have disappeared into anonymity.

The growth and success of these towns and the surrounding area began with a meeting held at the Red Lion Hotel in Caistor on 28th October 1844. Local landowners and other interested parties gathered to discuss proposals which had been put forward the previous month by a group of Sheffield businessmen, for the building of a railway connecting Grimsby with the proposed Sheffield & Lincolnshire Junction Railway at Gainsborough. The meeting, presided over by Lord Yarborough, unanimously passed the resolution to build the railway and agreed that a further meeting would be called to discuss the route. There was apparently a proposal to build a similar line in 1831 but nothing had come of it. The second meeting was held in the Town Hall in Grimsby on 6th November 1844 and on the agenda were three possible routes to Gainsborough, first via Caistor, a distance of 34¾ miles, second via Brigg (36½ miles) and third via Market Rasen (37¼

miles). The Brigg route was chosen whilst Caistor, which may well be said to have witnessed the birth of modern Grimsby, was forever to remain isolated from the railway system.

The new railway was to be known as the Great Grimsby and Sheffield Junction Railway and before the end of 1844 the GG&SJ had agreed with the Grimsby Haven Co. to form the Grimsby Docks Co.

A railway cannot be built without an act of parliament and the powers for the building of the GG&SJ was given royal assent on 30th June 1845. The act allowed for the building of a railway between Gainsborough and Grimsby with branches from Brigg – eventually built from Wrawby – to Market Rasen and from Habrough to New Holland at an estimated cost of £442,000. In reality however, the main line was built from Gainsborough to New Holland with a branch from Ulceby to Grimsby. At Ulceby, passengers for Grimsby would have to change trains, the only through trains to Grimsby from the west being specials for the passenger ships running from the port. It wasn't until 1888 that this situation changed when Grimsby and Cleethorpes became the easterly terminus of the main line and from that date passengers arriving from the west for New Holland and Hull had to change trains at Brocklesby. The contract for the building of the line was awarded to John Stephenson & Co. in the autumn of 1845.

In August 1845 the board of the GG&SJ agreed to purchase the ferries operating from Barrow, New Holland and Goxhill, these were purchased for £21,000 in October 1845. An act of parliament dated 26th June 1846 authorised the GG&SJ to operate steamboats across the Humber for the carriage of passengers and freight and this same act, incidentally, sanctioned the building of further branches from New Holland to Barton and from Grimsby to Cleethorpes. In 1850 it was discovered that a group of GG&SJ directors had in fact acquired the three ferries early in 1845 for only £10,000, so they were made to repay the difference to the company, and where applicable to relinquish their seats on the board of directors.

3. Grimsby c.1880. This view of the station staff at the east end of town station was probably taken about 1880. It is certainly before platform 3 was built and it is interesting to note the loading gauges at the departure end of both platforms, a legacy of the days when luggage was loaded on the roofs of carriages no doubt.

Photo: Grimsby Public Libraries

Grimsby however, was not acquiring just one railway but two, for although destined never to play a major role in the development of the area, the East Lincolnshire Railway had put forward plans to connect Grimsby and Louth with Boston and the formative Great Northern Railway, then known as the London and York. Until closure of through services in 1970 this line was to give Grimsby its most direct access to London and East Anglia. The act for the building of the line was passed on the same day as that for the GG&SJ Barton and Cleethorpes branches but before the act had been passed the GG&SJ approached the East Lincolnshire Railway with a suggestion that it be included in the proposed Manchester, Sheffield and Lincolnshire Railway. However, when royal assent was given to the formation of the MS&LR on the 27th July 1846, the name of the East Lincolnshire Railway was not included. The MS&L was subsequently formed from the amalgamation of the Sheffield, Ashton under Lyne and Manchester Railway, the Sheffield and Lincolnshire Junction Railway, the Great Grimsby and Sheffield Junction Railway, the Grimsby Docks Co. and several smaller railway and canal companies. The development of the MS&L into the Great Central Railway is well documented elsewhere but suffice it is to say that today the only major part of the GCR to survive, apart from the commuter services into and out of London, are the lines connecting Grimsby with Sheffield, Lincoln and Doncaster.

Determined not to allow another railway company access to Grimsby, the MS&L made an offer to the East Lincolnshire Railway in October 1846 to not only work the line between Grimsby and Louth but also to lease it. The Great Northern Railway however were equally determined to work the line and hopefully cream off some of the lucrative traffic the new works at Grimsby promised to generate. On the 4th February 1847 the East Lincolnshire Railway reached agreement with the GNR to operate the line although the ELR was to remain nominally independent until the grouping of the railways into the "Big Four" on 1st January 1923.

The original plans for the siting of a station in Grimsby can be deduced from the details of the route into the town proposed by the GG&SJ. *"Through the Great and Little Coates Lordships, onward to the Grimsby Little Field, where the course round the east side of the town commences, and then across the Friars and the paddock turnpike, etc., across Wellowgate, across the paddocks to the Starum lane end of Garden Street and onwards across Peppercorn six acres to midway of the East Marsh where a grand terminus will be erected."* Translated into modern terminology the above reads as via Great Coates, Little Coates, Littlefield Lane, Friargate, Wellowgate, Garden Street, Doughty Road (Peppercorn Walk) to the East Marsh, the original plans for a station being in the region of Duncombe Street. It is not known when the decision to site the station adjacent to the Old Market Place was taken but the East Lincolnshire Railway originally planned to run from Catherine Street to Pasture Street, the rather sharp curve from Catherine Street to Garden Street appearing to be an afterthought, although it was built in time for the opening of the line.

The eventual site chosen for Grimsby Town station was at the time the most sensible. Situated immediately behind the Market Place where the Town Hall was at the time, it was situated centrally for the then small population. The massive expansion of Grimsby in the latter half of the century however would have been much better catered for if, as already mentioned, the station had been built in the East Marsh.

The station buildings, substantial but never

luxurious, served two platforms with a bay at the eastern end of platform 1, which was later used for the Louth motor trains and ultimately for parcels traffic. From the outset the station had an overall roof with three tracks laid through the station. The two outer tracks served the platforms whilst the one in the centre was used for carriage storage. Early photographs show a locomotive pit for the inspection and oiling of the underside of motive power at the western end of platform 2. By the turn of the century a third platform had been added making the former platform 2 into an island platform. Avoiding lines for goods and excursion traffic were laid around the outside of the station at the same time, and facilities for the movement of cattle were provided between Wellowgate and Deansgate Bridge.

A locomotive depot was built between Newmarket Street and Grimsby Docks station on the eastern (Freeman Street) side of the line, though it has not been possible so far to trace the date these facilities were opened. The shed, of which few photographs or plans seem to exist, appeared to have had six covered tracks, each one probably having its own arched entrance. There was a coaling stage just south of the shed building and originally a turntable measuring 45 feet 10 inches, but this would appear to have been dismantled early in the 20th century. Due to the hard water in the area, the GCR were forced in 1898, to build a water softening plant, the first of its kind on the GCR. The importance of Grimsby loco diminished with the opening of the depot at Immingham in 1912, though in later years the shed was used for servicing the large fleet of shunting engines required at Grimsby and for

continued on page 8

4. Grimsby Town station from Wellowgate **circa 1900.**   *Photo: Grimsby Public Libraries*

5. Grimsby Town station entrance **circa 1900.**

Photo: Lens of Sutton

6. Barton-on-Humber, n.d. Barton on Humber station seen from the road in LNER days. For a single platform station the buildings are substantial and were obviously built with the prospect of the branch being extended and the line doubled. This never happened and the buildings were demolished in the 1970's and replaced by a bus shelter. *Photo: D. Lee Photography*

7. Habrough, c.1935. Habrough station was the only one of the original New Holland line stations not built to the standard pattern.

Looking along the down platform the non-standard layout of staggered platforms is readily apparent. Class J11 0-6-0 No. 5316 is entering the station with a New Holland – Cleethorpes train. *Photo: D. Thompson*

8. Grimsby Docks station, c.1910. MS&LR Sacré Class 6B 4-4-0 No. 4 is standing in the down platform with a New Holland – Cleethorpes train. The station buildings are on the left whilst in the left background part of the roof of Grimsby loco shed is visible. East Marsh sidings, on the right, are full of wagons and carriers carts and barrows are awaiting loading alongside the station entrance. *Photo: Lens of Sutton*

1: continued from page 6

servicing visiting locomotives that worked passenger and fish trains. By 1933 three of the tracks had lost their roof and sometime during the 1950's, the coaling stage, the roof over the remaining tracks and the eastern wall of the shed building, were demolished. The offices, along the western wall, were used until recently as a signing on point for drivers based at Grimsby but even this facility has now been withdrawn. The western and back walls of the shed still survive and the site is used by a coal merchant.

Although Deansgate Bridge was not finished until April 1848, the railways between Grimsby and New Holland and between Grimsby and Louth were completed by the end of February. Intermediate stations from New Holland, were built at Goxhill, Ulceby, Habrough, Stallingborough, Great Coates, Waltham & Humberstone, Holton-le-Clay & Tetney, North Thoresby and Ludborough. The original plans for the last four mentioned, all on the East Lincolnshire, would appear to have included an overall roof but in the event were built with staggered platforms on either side of a level crossing. The MS&L opened a further station at Thornton Curtis in November 1848 but replaced it in August 1849 with a new station a half mile closer to New Holland. The station adopted the name of some nearby monastic ruins and became known as Thornton Abbey. Before continuing it may well be useful to list other stations and halts opened between New Holland and Louth. Healing, opened on 1st April 1881, was built by Riggal and Hewins at a cost of £447. Hainton Street Halt (Welhome Road),

Weelsby Road Halt, Holton Village Halt, Grainsby, Utterby and Fotherby all opened on 11th December 1905. There had previously been a station at Fotherby, known as Fotherby Gatehouse, which was opened in February 1853 but closed on 28th June 1872.

To facilitate the transfer of passengers and goods at New Holland a pier 1500ft long was required, which extended straight out into the river and commenced at the northern end of New Holland Town station. At right angles to the end of the pier a jetty was built attached to a floating pontoon, enabling the passage between pier and ferry to be undertaken at any state of the tide. The pontoon was replaced in 1869 after the original one had sunk in a storm on the night of 18/19 October. That same storm, stated by one person to be the fiercest he could remember for at least 30 years, also breached the Cleethorpes branch for the first time. The railway along the pier was double track until, just before the terminus, the westernmost line swung outwards slightly to allow a third set of tracks for the storage of coal wagons for the ferries. After a fire in 1895 passengers had to cross the gap created by a pedestrian path and in 1915, the state of the structure caused heavy locomotives to be banned from the pier. Early in 1923 the pier closed to railway traffic whilst reconstruction took place, work which was completed in February 1928, subsequent rail services recommencing on the 19th March.

Daily traffic along the pier during its peak years averaged 30,000 passengers, 250 vehicles, 1,200 cattle and sheep and 300 tons of luggage
continued on page 10

9. New Holland, c.1978. An outstanding aerial view of New Holland taken in the late 1970's. The ferry on the left is the *Farringford* which came north in the mid 1970's after working on the Isle of Wight service. On the right is one of the last of the traditional coal burning Humber ferries, the *Wingfield Castle*. Since closure the *Farringford* has been scrapped but the *Wingfield Castle*, like her two sisters, *Tattershall* and *Lincoln Castles*, has survived. The *Lincoln Castle*, built in 1940, spent several years high and dry on the north bank of the river adjacent to the Humber Bridge before being bought by a local businessman and moved to Grimsby, being moored in the Old Dock where, since restoration, has been opened to the public as a bar and restaurant.

On the pier, coal wagons can be seen in the centre road and the point where the down line swung out to accommodate this siding is clearly visible. Like New Holland Town, the Pier station once had an overall roof and there was a cattle dock on the pier adjacent to the river end of the buildings on the down platform. Beyond Town station the New Holland triangle is visible with the Grimsby line swinging away first left then right before heading in a straight line for Goxhill.

The dock is heavily silted but is still in regular use whilst behind it the timber pond is out of use and partially dried up. *Photo: Grimsby Evening Telegraph*

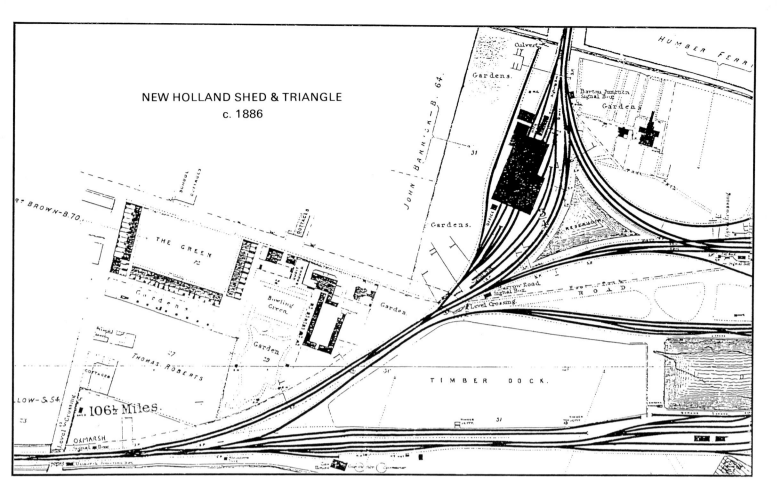

NEW HOLLAND SHED & TRIANGLE
c. 1886

10. New Holland Pier, 28th April 1928. This view was taken just one month after the pier re-opened to rail traffic after undergoing major reconstruction. The platforms/walkways have been retimbered and the platform facings have been remade in concrete. The major part of the reconstruction work however was to the main structure which carried the pier out into the river. Class D9 4-4-0 No. 6024 stands in the middle road awaiting the arrival of a train from Cleethorpes.

Photo: D. Lee Photography

1: continued from page 8

and goods although these figures do not take into account the additional traffic at holiday times.

New Holland Town station had two platforms bisected by four tracks. Substantial station buildings were provided on the eastern platform and there was overall roofing at one time, both here and at the Pier station, although there is no record of when they were demolished. To the east of the station was a small dock, some 600ft long by 200ft wide, plus a timber pond, since filled in, at the southern end, which was protected from the main dock by sluice gates. There were three 2 ton hydraulic cranes along the east quay and there was also a similar 12 ton crane on the west quay at one time. Originally the west quay accommodated three hydraulic shutes which were used for loading salt and at a later date, coal, a commodity used by the Royal Navy and loaded here for Gibraltar. In 1897 the centre shute was dismantled and replaced by a hydraulic coal hoist, itself dismantled in May and June 1949. The dock was at one time, served by as many as ten sidings on its western side with a similar number on the eastern side serving both the dock and the timber pond.

To the south of the Town station was a triangle of lines formed by the Grimsby – New Holland, Grimsby – Barton and New Holland – Barton routes. In the centre of the triangle was a reservoir which supplied water to the locomotive depot and the station. Alongside the southern arm of the triangle the MS&LR built a locomotive shed, which had four tracks, each with its own arched entrance beneath a roof of two arches. Until 1941, New Holland had a small allocation of locomotives, but afterwards the engines were supplied by Immingham. It was always possible to see at least one and often several locos on the shed until the diesel multiple units took charge of the passenger workings in the late 1950's. Latterly two of the archways were knocked into one and the shed partially rebuilt but by 1960 it was roofless and played host to a solitary diesel shunter. However, it has since been demolished, although it is of interest to note that, in 1865, wagon repairs were being carried out at the shed in the open as there was no room under cover, a most unpleasant duty when one considers how the wind can whip off the nearby River Humber at times.

Train movements were controlled by five signal boxes, Oxmarsh Junction, Barrow Road Crossing, New Holland Town and New Holland Pier with Barton Junction at the western end of the triangle. This box disappeared many years ago and latterly New Holland Pier box was out of use. Today, movements are controlled by a new Oxmarsh Junction and the original Barrow Road. New Holland Town box has since been demolished as has the fine station of the same name

although New Holland Pier box can still be seen at the end of the pier.

To accommodate the staff needed to operate its installations the railway company built a series of cottage homes known as Manchester Square and which still survive. Attached to the rear of the Yarborough Hotel, now known as the Lincoln Castle, was a laundry which served all the stations and hotels in the area. In GCR days it performed the same service for places as far away as Manchester. The hotel was opened in April 1851 and replaced the original Yarborough Arms Hotel, being built by Wm. Kirk of Lincoln. It cost £1,825.

The railways, between Grimsby and New Holland and Grimsby and Louth opened simultaneously on 1st March 1848 with the MS&L and GNR operating a New Holland – Louth service on a 50/50 basis. This system continued until July 1851 when events elsewhere in the railway world caused friction between the two companies to such an extent that the MS&L placed blocks on the line at Garden Street and were known to have despatched the last ferry from New Holland before the arrival of the last Great Northern train, thereby stranding passengers for Hull on the south bank overnight. There are also reports of fights with fists and weapons between employees of the two companies when the GNR tried to forcibly remove the obstructions at Garden Street. It is only fair to state that the GNR were very much the innocent party in these sad affairs. The London and North Western Railway, with whom the MS&L were closely allied at the time, was fearful of losing a lot of traffic to the GNR when its main line to the north opened and therefore persuaded its allies to be as obstructive as possible towards the GNR. The outcome of all this in the Grimsby area was the loss of through trains between New Holland and Louth as from the 9th July 1851. The GNR did try to maintain its services by going through the courts but to no avail and ever after passengers from the East Lincolnshire line would have to change at Grimsby when travelling to New Holland and Hull.

On 29th February, 1848, the day before the railway opened, a party of MS&L directors set out from Hull in one of the two newly acquired paddle steamers to visit New Holland and have a tour of the newly completed line. After taking breakfast at the Yarborough Arms they set out by train from New Holland at 10 a.m., arriving at Grimsby at 10.45 a.m. where they met local dignitaries before proceeding to Louth. It would appear that they were joined at Louth by directors and guests of the East Lincolnshire Railway for the return journey and all went well until, when nearing New Holland, two carriages became derailed. So substantial was the coaching stock of the day that the passengers

continued on page 16

11. Healing, August 1961. Healing was the last of the stations on the New Holland line to be opened, in 1881, until New Holland Halt replaced the Town and Pier stations 100 years later. Comparison of this August 1961 view with the other stations along the line shows how building designs had simplified, almost to the austere, in the years since 1848. The main buildings are on the up platform and have been extended with the addition of a wooden waiting room. On the down platform there is a brick built waiting room dating from 1881 which has been supplemented with a wooden structure not unlike a greenhouse. Healing signal box, the first along this stretch of line to close, is about to be passed by a Class K3 on a semi-fast train for Cleethorpes.   *Photo: G. Biddle*

12. Great Coates, n.d. Great Coates is the first station out of Grimsby on the New Holland line and today comes within the borough boundary. The station buildings are of standard New Holland line design with the main buildings on the up platform. The effect of a train travelling through this station at speed is an experience as the down platform appears to bounce, suggesting that it is built on fairly marshy land.

Photo: Welholme Galleries

13. Ludborough, c.1905. An up train is approaching Ludborough station hauled by one of H. A. Ivatts large boilered Atlantics. Comparison with the view of North Thoresby shows the similarity of construction. Holton le Clay and Waltham were also almost identical. *Photo: Courtesy GLRPS*

14. Utterby Halt, c.1910. One of the GNR railmotors, either no. 5 or no. 6, waits at the low platform with a Grimsby–Louth train. The driver is in the compartment at this end of the train, control being from this point.

Photo: Courtesy GLRPS

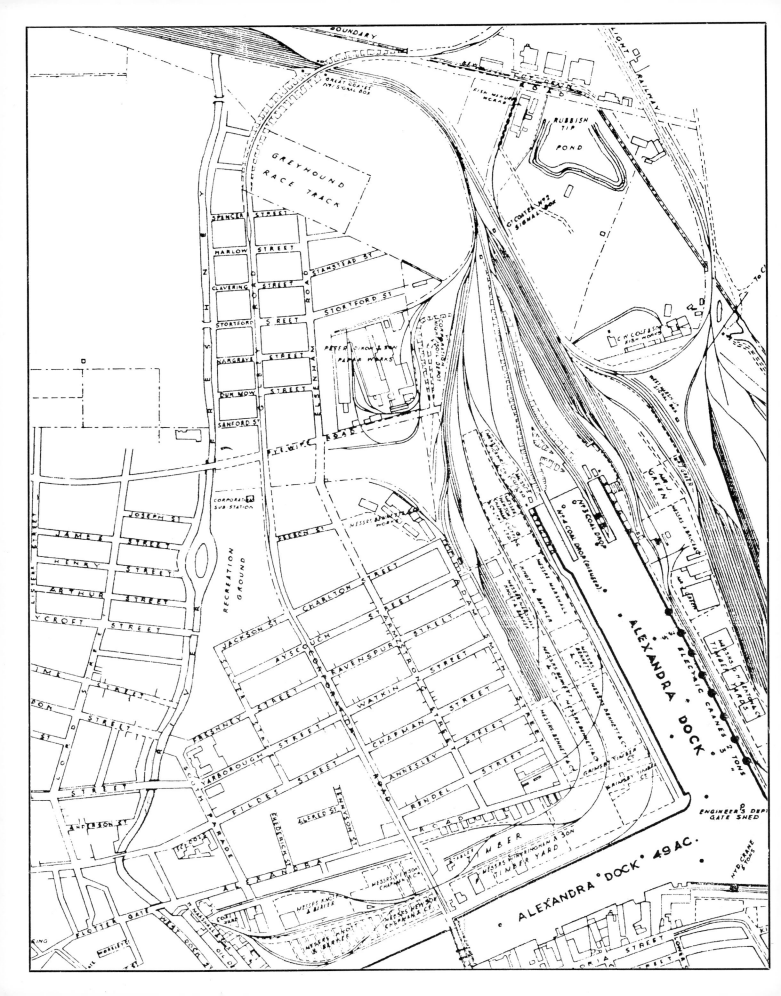

GRIMSBY DOCKS

Stations and Offices	RED
Warehouses and Sheds	
Cranes	●
Coaling Appliances	▬
Quays	THICK LINE
Sheer Legs	△

— SCALE —

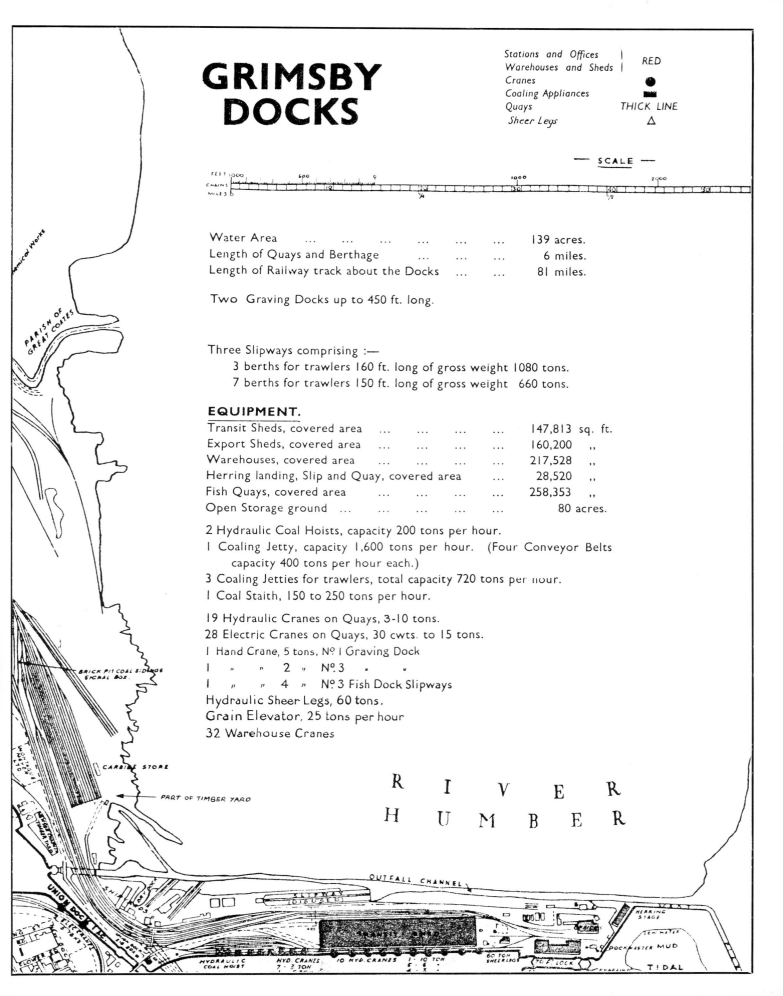

Water Area	139 acres.
Length of Quays and Berthage	6 miles.
Length of Railway track about the Docks	81 miles.

Two Graving Docks up to 450 ft. long.

Three Slipways comprising :—
    3 berths for trawlers 160 ft. long of gross weight 1080 tons.
    7 berths for trawlers 150 ft. long of gross weight 660 tons.

EQUIPMENT.

Transit Sheds, covered area	147,813 sq. ft.
Export Sheds, covered area	160,200 ,,
Warehouses, covered area	217,528 ,,
Herring landing, Slip and Quay, covered area ...	28,520 ,,
Fish Quays, covered area	258,353 ,,
Open Storage ground	80 acres.

2 Hydraulic Coal Hoists, capacity 200 tons per hour.
1 Coaling Jetty, capacity 1,600 tons per hour. (Four Conveyor Belts
    capacity 400 tons per hour each.)
3 Coaling Jetties for trawlers, total capacity 720 tons per hour.
1 Coal Staith, 150 to 250 tons per hour.

19 Hydraulic Cranes on Quays, 3-10 tons.
28 Electric Cranes on Quays, 30 cwts. to 15 tons.
1 Hand Crane, 5 tons, No. 1 Graving Dock
1 ,, ,, 2 ,, No. 3 ,, ,,
1 ,, ,, 4 ,, No. 3 Fish Dock Slipways
Hydraulic Sheer Legs, 60 tons.
Grain Elevator, 25 tons per hour
32 Warehouse Cranes

R I V E R

H U M B E R

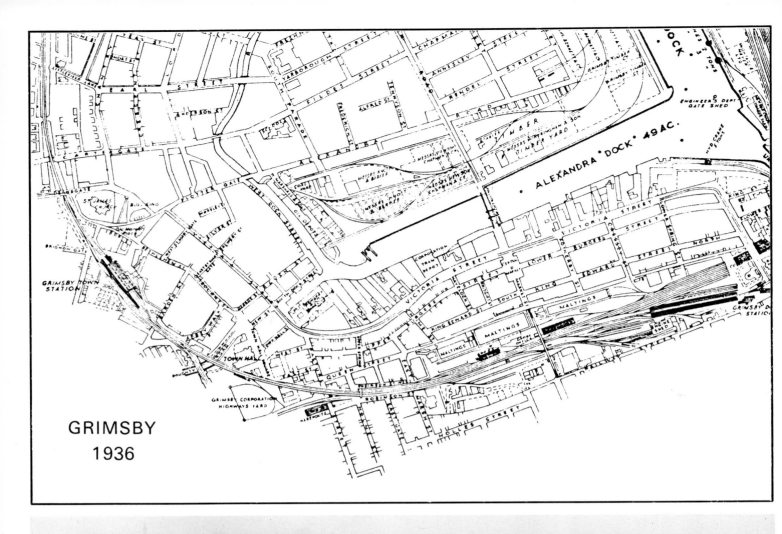

GRIMSBY
1936

15. Grimsby GN Goods, Pasture Street, c.1930. Obviously taken in the days before the passing of the Clean Air Act, probably circa 1930, a pall of smoke and fumes is hanging over the East Marsh and almost obscuring the Dock Tower in the distance. In the foreground is the roof of Goods Junction signal box, burnt down by vandals in the 1970's, whilst in the centre the goods yard is a hive of activity as scores of wagons await their turn for loading or unloading. Today the site is occupied by DIY and electrical superstores whilst the photographers vantage point appears to be one of the, now demolished, buildings at the electricity works.

Photo: H. L. Lowe courtesy GLRPS

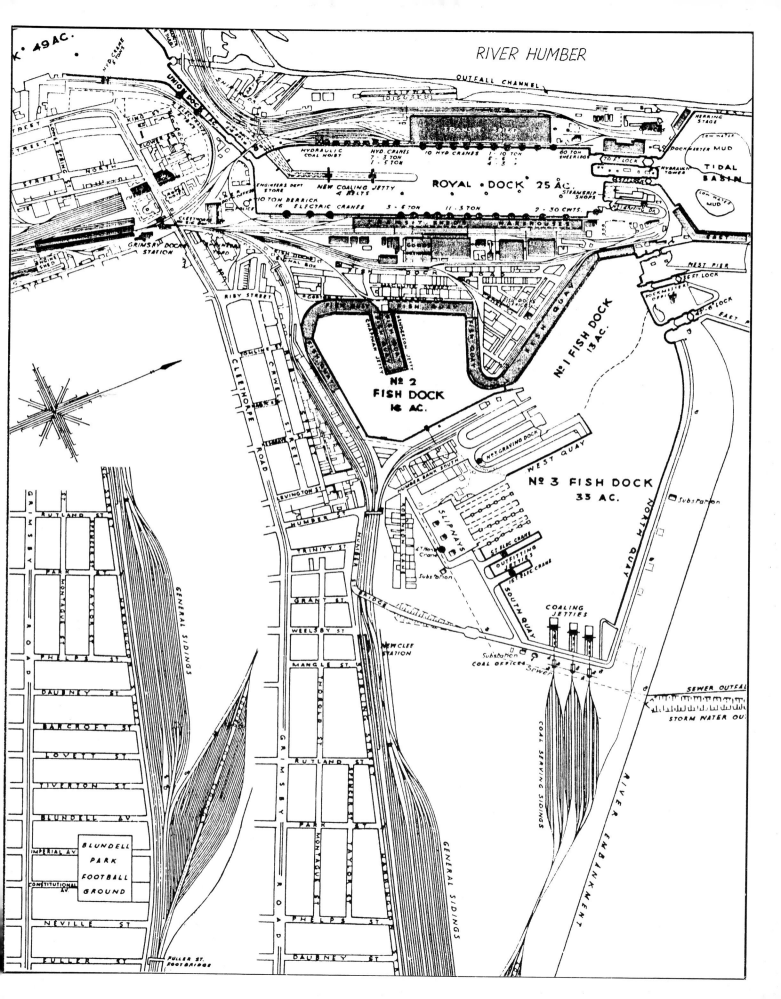

1: continued from page 10

climbed out, levered the carriages back onto the track, returned to their seats and continued on their journey.

The main line between Ulceby and Brigg and the Market Rasen branch from Wrawby Junction opened on 1st November 1848. There were two intermediate stations, Brocklesby and Barnetby, the former built mainly for the use of the Worsley family, having seen numerous Royal visitors who have stayed the night at Brocklesby Hall, before attending functions in the area. Because of the number of VIP's expected to pass through its portals, Brocklesby station was built to a very ornate design whereas Barnetby, which served a much larger community, was austere by comparison. Refreshment rooms were opened at both Barnetby and Ulceby in 1855. A small, two road engine shed was built in the fork of the Brigg and Market Rasen lines at Wrawby Junction. Constructed by Logan and Hemingway at a cost of £4,450 in the mid 1870's it included a turntable and coaling facilities. The depot probably closed around 1932 when the new depot at Frodingham opened although it was originally under the control of Immingham MPD and, therefore, could be considered as losing its independence from the opening of the latter depot.

In 1861 the MS&LR joined forces with the South Yorkshire Railway to assist in promoting the Trent, Ancholme and Grimsby Railway along with Roland Winn and George and William Dawes. This line, with a capital of £120,000, was authorised to construct a railway from Keadby, on the western bank of the Trent, via Frodingham, Appleby

and Elsham to a junction with the MS&LR at Wrawby. Although aimed primarily at tapping the iron ore deposits in the area it also gave the Grimsby area a vital link into the rail network of South and West Yorkshire. The line opened on the 1st May 1866 and actually joined the Brigg line a few yards to the west of its junction with the Market Rasen line. The three lines diverging at this point have been known by generations of railwaymen as, from south to north, Lincoln branch, Main line and Yorkshire branch.

The branch to Barton opened on the 1st March 1849 and the intermediate halt at Barrow Haven followed on 2nd April 1850. Although authorised at the same time the Cleethorpes branch was destined not to materialise until 1863.

The major factor in building a railway to Grimsby was to exploit its potential as a port. By far the greatest influence on the future economy of the area was the formation on 8th August 1845 of the Grimsby Dock Co., which took over the old Grimsby Haven Co. originally formed in 1796 to build a dock which eventually became known as the Old Dock. In later years it was to become the southerly arm of the Alexandra Dock, stretching from Lock Hill to the Riverhead. Although it was a boost to trade in its early years, the 1840's saw business dwindle and the deep water channel show signs of silting up. Help was sorely needed, and help came in the form of the aforementioned Grimsby Dock Co. which was so closely allied to the GG&SJ that five directors were on both boards. The Grimsby Dock Co. proposed a new dock slightly to

16. Brocklesby, n.d. In this fine view of Brocklesby station the 4.45pm Nottingham fish train, hauled by ex LMS Class 5MT 4-6-0 44861, is incidental when compared with the handsome Tudor style architecture of the station building. Opened in 1848 the station was built principally for the use of the Worsley family and their visitors, which sometimes included members of the Royal family. It was the Worsley family, through their head, Lord Yarborough, who were instrumental in bringing the railways to the area. This was reflected in the composition of the MS&L board of directors which for many years included a member of the family.
Photo: C. J. Paine

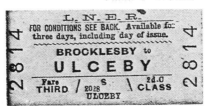

17. Barnetby, c.1910. A damaged but nonetheless interesting view of the western approach to Barnetby taken before the rebuilding of 1912. One of J. G. Robinson's handsome Atlantics No. 263 is entering the station with a stopping train for Cleethorpes whilst a 0-6-0 can be seen busily marshalling a goods train in the yards in the background. The platform on the right was soon to disappear with the rebuilding leaving the station building isolated from the platforms.
Photo: Courtesy Grimsby-Louth RPS

the east of the Old Dock, which would extend ¾ of a mile out into the river and cover 20 acres together with a further 13 acres in a tidal basin. In all 138 acres of land were to be reclaimed from the Humber. Two sets of lock pits were built 300 feet long, the larger being 70 feet wide and the smaller 45 feet wide, hydraulic water pressure being used to open the lock gates with the water being contained 200 feet above ground in a 33,000 gallon tank. This tank was enclosed in a brick tower similar in design to an Italian campanile at Sienna. The building is better known today as Grimsby's outstanding landmark, "The Dock Tower". The hydraulic pressure provided by the tower was also used in opening and closing Cleethorpe Road level crossing. Similar but smaller towers later appeared alongside the large lock pit and on the east side of no. 2 Fish Dock, the latter undoubtedly for operating the gates of the graving dock opened nearby in 1875.

In 1854 a six acre fish dock adjacent to the north east corner of the Royal Dock was authorised, and as Grimsby was already beginning to attract fishermen from other parts of the country, a dock specifically designed for the fishing trade was desperately needed, being completed two years later. By the end of 1863 the building of the Royal Dock – including two coal drops and a graving dock built in the intervening years – and the Fish Dock, plus the purchase of the Old Dock, had involved the MS&L in a total investment of more than £1,000,000, an outlay that in the few years the docks had been in existence was already paying handsome dividends in the amount of goods and passenger traffic being generated. A grain warehouse on the east side of the Royal Dock was added in 1879 and a large transit shed was built on the west side in 1893. Together with the necessary sidings, a further coal hoist which was situated in the south west corner of the Royal Dock was brought into use in 1899.

On the 18th April 1849 Brocklesby station saw the first of several royal visitors when, after spending the previous night with Lord Yarborough, Prince Albert boarded a special train for Grimsby. Arriving in Grimsby around 1 p.m. the train passed under a triumphal arch before entering the station. Here, the Prince was welcomed by the Mayor and other civic dignitaries before resuming his rail journey towards the docks. The train passed under two more triumphal arches before arriving at the dock entrance where the locomotive was uncoupled. The royal train was then pulled into the dock area by 100 very smartly dressed navvies. The Prince then proceeded to lay the foundation stone of the new dock in what was to become one of the two lock pits. After wishing the venture every success and accepting several loyal toasts on behalf of the Queen, the Prince left Grimsby, travelling back to London via Louth and Boston.

Work on the new dock was completed by the 18th March 1852 when the contractors, Hutchings, Brown & Wright, gave a banquet in the bottom of the larger of the lock pits. Four days later water was admitted to the dock for the first time and two months later on 27th May it was brought into public use. The railway connecting the docks with Grimsby Town station however was not completed until the 1st August 1853 when two more stations, Grimsby Docks and Pier, were brought into use. One must assume therefore that Prince Albert must have travelled, at least in part, over the contractors railway. On the 14th October 1854 the new dock was given the royal seal of approval when, on her way back to London after a holiday in Scotland, and an overnight stay in Hull, Queen Victoria landed at Grimsby from the Royal yacht. She was received by Lord Yarborough, the Mayor, and the Corporation. The MS&L requested, in a loyal address, that in order to honour the visit of Her Royal Majesty to Grimsby, permission be given to call the new dock, the Royal Dock. This request was graciously granted and so the name by which the dock is known to this day came into being. The Royal party then departed in a procession through the streets of Grimsby to the Town station where they boarded the Great Northern Railway's Royal train to complete their journey to London.

On the 21st August 1849 Edward Watkin and Adam Smith of the MS&L met with the Freemen of Grimsby to discuss the extension of the railway to Cleethorpes authorised in 1846. The railway company proposed a line running north from the East Marsh until it reached the coast and then following the shoreline into Cleethorpes. They also offered to build an ornamental footbridge from the New (Central) Market over the railway to the East Marsh, this bridge eventually being built in 1871. They declined a request from the Freemen to build a carriage way across the lines at this point as seven tracks already existed and more were planned. A promise was also made to build a station in the East Marsh in addition to the one already planned at Grimsby Docks. Not for the last time was the East Marsh promised a station and

equally not for the last time was the station not to materialise. The two representatives, however were willing to accept any proposals the Freemen may have wished to make for an alternative route and several proposals were put forward without anything coming of them.

In 1855 the question of a line to Cleethorpes arose again. Probably based on the 1849 suggestions by the Freemen the railway company put forward three proposals, one being to leave the railway on the Pasture Street side of Kent Street cross Freeman Street and run along Church Street and Brereton Avenue, a second along Nelson Street, across Freeman Street, then skirting the northern edge of Freeman Street Market, proceed along Garibaldi Street and cross Hope Street, Victor Street, Tunnard Street, and Park Street to Sidney Park and on into the heart of Cleethorpes. The third would route the railway along Holme Street and Clyde Street, across Freeman Street and Convamore Road to Grant Thorold Park, entering Cleethorpes close to Fiveways.

For those who know that part of town it will be abundantly clear that any of the proposed routes would have had a disastrous effect on the traffic flow in the East Marsh. Thankfully, once again these proposals came to nought, otherwise the east side of Grimsby would have been as bedevilled with level crossings as is the west side of the town.

At this point it may be worthwhile to look at the position of the level crossings on either side of Newmarket Street footbridge. Entering Grimsby from the west are encountered Littlefield Lane, Friargate, Wellowgate, Garden Street, Pasture Street and Holme Street, all in a total distance of less than ¾ mile. The shortest distance between any of these crossings was the 80 yards between Pasture Street and Holme Street whilst the longest distance was the 466 yards between Garden Street and Pasture Street which, before the building of Doughty Road subway – built in 1895 at a cost of £7,000 – contained a further crossing, for pedestrians only, about 150 yards from Garden Street at Peppercorn Walk. This crossing, before its replacement, was the scene of several accidents including at least one fatality. Grimsby Town station lay between Wellowgate and Garden Street, the whole of the station being built within a length of 288 yards. With station limits being so tight several trains a day would block one of the level crossings during their time at the station, probably the best known of these being Cleethorpes to Kings Cross trains which even today, when operated by High Speed Trains, causes this practice to continue. To the east is Cleethorpe Road, once claimed to be the busiest level crossing in the country with over 900 train movements a day, and Fish Dock Road. There is also the crossing at Suggitts Lane in Cleethorpes but there can be few people who have ever seen this crossing used by road traffic.

Cleethorpes was obviously a goal the MS&L had set its sights upon and in 1861 a further application to build the line was made. Gone were the crazy proposals of 1855 and in their place was basically the MS&L proposal of 1849. This time Cleethorpes was at last to get the railway and after some difficulty with local landowners, construction commenced. The line, single track throughout, opened on 6th April 1863, but it wasn't until 1874 that it became double track. The only intermediate station on the branch, New Clee, opened on 1st July 1875. Thirty years later a halt was opened for dock workers at Fish Dock Road, this halt being known as Riby Street Platforms.

In 1880 plans were made to improve the station facilities, a move that proved to be fortuitous. The original station buildings, which still survive today, were built on what is now no. 1 platform. The 1880 modernisation placed new station buildings across the platform ends, the number of platforms increased to six and a turntable installed adjacent to the station signal box. Early in the 20th century this measured 65ft, larger than the one at Grimsby.

However, before these improvements were put into operation the MS&L was asked if it was prepared to undertake the protection and preservation of the coastline at Cleethorpes and this they agreed to do. As a result, 17 acres of land were acquired in 1882 and in the following year the improvements commenced.

The sea wall was built in 1883, followed a year later by the acquisition of the pier company whose structure had been built as long ago as 1872. By the 2nd July 1885, when Prince Albert Victor performed a public opening, swimming baths, a restaurant, collonade and refreshment rooms had been provided. Gardens were landscaped and the promenade provided with lighting. Later in the decade a grotto was built in the cliff gardens and a pavilion provided at the pier head.

More extensions to the sea wall were started in 1891 and a further 33 acres of land, the only part of the foreshore between High Cliff, Cleethorpes and Pyewipe, west of Grimsby, not under MS&L ownership, was acquired in 1892.

As the century closed the bill the MS&L had paid for Cleethorpes was over £100,000 but visitors now came in their thousands. Seventeen years had gone by from the passing of the first act to build a line to Cleethorpes in 1846 to its actual construction. A further seventeen then passed before the railway company began to invest any amount of money in the town but surely the sum of £100,000 +, when finally invested, was some of the most profitable the company ever spent, especially when one considers that the resort was reporting as many as 30,000 visitors a day on occasions.

Finally, to emphasise the importance of Cleethorpes to the MS&L, let us consider Whitsun 1888. An epidemic of smallpox had broken out at Grimsby and in fact cases were being reported as close to Cleethorpes as New Clee. All special trains were at first cancelled but, after a public outcry, reinstated albeit running non stop through Grimsby.

Except for a partial improvement to and enlargement of the Fish Docks in the late 1860's there were no major dock works carried out until 1873, with the decision to make a new dock connecting the Old and Royal Docks, the reason for this being to provide more quay space for the ever-increasing shipping. It is also possible the decision was taken due to severe silting of the creek leading to the lock in the Old Dock. Constructed by Logan & Hemingway and costing £81,000, it was completed in 1879 and became known as the Union Dock. The official opening was carried out on the 22nd of July by the Prince and Princess of Wales, the Royal couple having travelled through the new dock on board one of the New Holland – Hull paddle steamers. During the visit

the Chairman of the MS&L, Sir Edward Watkin, presented to the town the statue of Prince Albert, which for many years stood facing the Royal Hotel. When Cleethorpe Road flyover was built in the mid 1960's the statue was moved to its present position facing the Dock Offices, built in 1885. Obviously the prince prefers the view to that of the flyover and who can blame him? The base of the statue records the opening of the Royal and Union docks together with extracts from the prince Consort's speech of 1849, when he laid the foundation stone of the Royal Dock. The name of the donor also appears.

Only months after authorising the construction of the Union Dock it became apparent that demand would soon outstrip the capacity of the available quay space, including the new dock. More facilities were desperately needed so the MS&L instructed its Consulting Engineer, Charles Liddell, to look at possible sites. His report, submitted in the spring of 1874, suggested a site to the west of Grimsby at Killingholme. A saving of £250,000 could be made if a new dock was built here rather than at Grimsby. In addition the deep water channel was a mere 300 yards from the shoreline at Killingholme whereas at Grimsby the distance was in the region of 1500 yards. Logically the choice should have fallen upon Killingholme but somewhat surprisingly the MS&L purchased 105 acres of land in the West Marsh from Grimsby Corporation and, for the time being, the Killingholme scheme faded quietly away.

In June 1876, Logan and Hemingway, a name that became synonymous with new works for the MS&L, were awarded a contract to

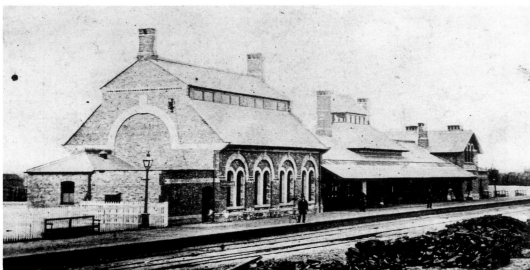

18. Cleethorpes, c.1875. The original station at Cleethorpes in the 1870's. The substantial buildings served a single platform until the rebuilding in the 1880's when the station was extended to its present size and new buildings erected. However the original buildings were not even twenty years old when this happened and they have survived to the present day, now being used as a pub and a club.

Photo: Welholme Galleries

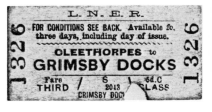

19. Cleethorpes, May 1965. The proof of the pudding! The original station buildings in May 1965 showing little change from the photograph above. A water tank has been added at the far end and attic windows built into the roof of what is now the No. 1 Refreshment Rooms. There has also been some realignment to the roofline of the main part of the building. Standing in platform 1 are two sets of Derby built Class 114 DMU's. Introduced in 1956 these vehicles spent almost their entire lives based at Lincoln and became a familar part of the railway scene in the area until their replacement by newer units in 1987.

Photo: R. E. G. Read courtesy G. Biddle

20. Cleethorpes, c.1911. Crowds surge along platform 6 at Cleethorpes in 1911 to sample the delights the resort has to offer whilst the fireman of their train pulls coal forward in the tender of his Class J10 0-6-0. Looking along the seafront it is quite unfamiliar to visitors of today being devoid of amusement arcades and the big wheel and even those once familiar, but now no more, landmarks such as the Big Dipper and Hawkeys Cafe.

Photo: GCRS

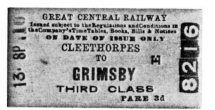

construct No. 2 Fish Dock covering 11 acres and costing £23,000. This extension to the fish dock was built between the original No. 1 Fish Dock and the Cleethorpes branch. In 1894 this dock was extended to 16 acres and two coal hoists were built on its eastern side for bunkering trawlers. This extension was the cause of the severe reverse curves on the Cleethorpes branch between Fish Dock Road and Humber Street as the original route of the line was required for the construction of the new quays.

When the Union Dock was authorised in 1873 provision was made for the construction of a branch line joining the west side of the Royal Dock to the main line west of Grimsby. The need for this line is evident when it is considered that until the building of the Union Dock, access to the west side of the Royal Dock was gained from Grimsby Docks station, a route that would be severed by the construction of the new dock. Restricted rail access by means of a swing bridge was available after the dock was built, but did not have the capacity to take the number of trains using the west side of the dock.

Opened on 27th March 1879 the great Coates branch was approximately two miles long and would appear to have left the main line somewhere near the present day Marsh Junction. The branch ran parallel to the main line for a short distance before swinging north along what is now Boulevard Avenue. It then swung east into the maze of sidings that at one time lay between the Alexandra Dock and the Humber bank. Although closed for many years the remains of the piles for the bridge over the Freshney can still be seen alongside todays road bridge. It wasn't until the 1960's that the gatehouse at the crossing of Armstrong Street was demolished, having stood in the corner of Peter Dixons paper mills car park. Within a few years of its opening the branch carried the majority of coal exported through Grimsby and around this time several sidings were laid along the north side of Healing station, presumably for holding incoming coal trains. It is possible, although unconfirmed, that sidings were laid in a similar position at Stallingborough.

Construction of the Great Coates branch had commenced in 1878 and it was towards the end of that year that the MS&L accepted a proposal from Logan and Hemingway to build a new dock extending westwards from the northern end of the Old Dock and covering 26 of the 105 acres purchased some four years earlier. Completed in July 1880 and costing around £55,000 the new dock together with the Old Dock were named the Alexandra Dock in honour of the aforementioned visit by the Prince and Princess of Wales. Shortly after completion a further £45,000 was authorised for the construction of two coal drops – at the western end of the dock – and some timber jetties and cranes and the Union Dock swing bridge referred to earlier. An additional coal drop costing £13,000 was added during the 1880's. When the railways reached their zenith in Grimsby during the 20th century there were 81 miles of track on the dock estate, 6 miles of which served quaysides.

By the end of the 19th century the coming of the railway had radically changed the fortunes of Grimsby and Cleethorpes. For instance, 100 years previously the population of Grimsby had been less than 1,000 but by 1841 it had risen to 3,700 before more than doubling in the next

ten years to 8,860. By 1901 that figure had reached 75,000. Not all of these people, it is true, worked for the railway, although the MS&L were the largest employer in the town. However, without the rail outlets and dock facilities provided by the company there would have been no reason for people to move to the area.

In little more than 50 years, in Grimsby alone, the MS&L had built three commercial docks and renovated a fourth, two fish docks, three stations and a locomotive depot. Goods facilities were catered for in the large yards at East Marsh and Alexandra Dock – better known as Brickpit Sidings – plus a myriad of short lines around the docks serving individual businesses. One of these small lines left the East Marsh sidings and travelled along Cressey Street crossing King Edward Street, Burgess Street and Victoria Street. It is believed that for this line at least, the motive power was provided by a horse. In 1926 GGST tram no. 27 was hit by a wagon which broke loose on this short section of line and ran back across Victoria Street. Fortunately there appears to have been no serious injuries and the tram was soon returned to service. Goods sheds existed either side of Newmarket Street footbridge (MS&L) and at Pasture Street (GNR). The GNR had actually built an extensive goods yard here including a cattle dock and a locomotive pit for servicing its locomotives. The Gas and Electric companies were also served by sidings just to the south of Pasture Street goods depot and the Royal Dock in particular, was surrounded by transit sheds, warehouses and grain silos.

Besides its large investment in the railway and docks at Grimsby the MS&L had also purchased the two large hotels in the town in 1890. These were the Yarborough, built 1853, and the Royal, formerly known as the Royal Dock Hotel, built in 1863.

Other ventures in which the MS&L had involved itself included the Deep Sea Fishing Co., which it formed jointly with the Great Northern Railway and the Midland Railway in May 1854. This enterprise soon owned nine vessels and was really the bedrock upon which the ports deep water fleet was built. Two years later the MS&L along with the South Yorkshire Railway, which in later years became part of the MS&L, and some French businessmen, formed the Anglo-French Steamship Co. Ten years later the MS&L wholly owned this company.

In operation mainly to carry coal to France, the Anglo-French soon began to build up a varied range of continental services. There were regular sailings from Grimsby to Hamburg, Rotterdam, Antwerp and many other ports. One outcome of the Antwerp service was that in 1895, when there were three sailings a week between the ports, the mighty Cunard line would despatch its Antwerp – New York cargo by MS&L steamer to Grimsby, transport it by rail to Liverpool and then load it onto one of their own ships for onward passage to New York, a process which was four days quicker than sending it all the way by sea. Human cargo, in the form of emigrants from all over Europe, also passed through Grimsby in their thousands on their way to Liverpool and a new life in the United States. Indeed, so many passed through the port that shortly after its opening, Grimsby Pier station closed and became a transitional home for emigrants. The ships that operated

continued on page 21

21. Grimsby, Alexandra Dock. c.1955. The last of the commercial docks to be built in Grimsby was the western arm of the Alexandra Dock. When this photograph was taken in the 1950's however, the dock was almost 75 years old. Once extremely busy there is ample evidence that it is gradually falling into disuse. The coal jetties at the west end of the dock are no more than skeletal remains and the dock is in use as a timber pond. In fact the dock is, and until recently still was, surrounded by timber sheds. It eventually became almost derelict until recently when a car terminal was built at its western end and the section of the Old Dock from Union Dock to Corporation Bridge, out of view top right, became a marina.

Along the north side of the dock is Brick Pit sidings with Great Coates sidings at its western end. The Grimsby District Railway is just visible as it takes a 180 degree curve from Great Coates sidings around to Pyewipe Road. Peter Dixons paper mill is in the bottom right corner with the gatehouse, where the original Great Coates branch crossed Armstrong Street, just visible to the right of the pulp stacks. Immediately above these pulp stacks and adjacent to a saw mill, is Adam Smith Street signing on point, the water tower, under which was the enginemans bothy, being just visible.

Note the hundreds of open wagons in the sidings all around the dock. All that remains, in railway terms, is part of Brick Pit sidings which still sees regular use for steel traffic, and the Grimsby District Railway, now single track. The A180 trunk road now runs through the right centre of the view and if it were not for the docks a similar view today would be hardly recognisable by comparison.

Photo: E. Green

1: continued from page 19

these services were typical of the day but in the latter part of the century, with new ships entering service, they began to earn a reputation for safety and comfort. Not so stylish, but representative of places served by the company, were the names of these ships. Leeds, Sheffield, Manchester, Huddersfield, Staveley and Lutterworth being typical of the names used by the MS&L.

Perhaps the final words on the development of Grimsby and Cleethorpes should be left to the company that performed the work, these two quotes being taken from the Great Central Railway Official Album.

Of Grimsby, by "the Mariner" from a series of articles on ports of the U.K. "*The Manchester, Sheffield and Lincolnshire Railway found Grimsby in the depths of despair, and they have raised it up to a high pitch of exultancy at things achieved and of hope for things to be achieved in the future. Nor is this any great wonder. Connecting Grimsby directly with the salt mines of Cheshire and the richest coal districts of South Yorkshire, the railway company, from these sources alone, has sufficient store to foster any port that they might choose to open; and when it is remembered that Grimsby is undoubtedly the port above all others adapted for the trade between the Midlands and Eastern parts of England and the Northern ports of Europe, it will readily be understood how, with a powerful company, well furnished with the sinews of trade to back it, it has at length recovered all of and more than its ancient prosperity. But besides the two great sources of wealth referred to above, the Manchester, Sheffield and Lincolnshire Railway Co. are in touch with all the principal manufacturing towns of the central belt of the United Kingdom: Barrow, Birmingham, Derby, Doncaster, Halifax, Huddersfield, Leeds, Liverpool, Manchester, Nottingham, Peterborough, Sheffield, Wakefield, Warrington, all avail themselves of the facilities for the shortest transit to the Baltic and North Sea ports; nor does London itself disdain to look upon Grimsby as a useful outlet for much of its merchandise; while to all the great towns and to the capitol itself, Grimsby, as a feeder from foreign ports, is invaluable.*"

Of Cleethorpes. "*Beyond Grimsby the line has been pushed to Cleethorpes, a village once inhabited by a few fishermen only in winter, but now changed by a unique effort of railway enterprise into the most crowded watering place in Lincolnshire. It is almost entirely the property of the Great Central Railway, who have built there a massive sea wall, 65 feet wide, the inner side of which is a broad carriage drive, divided from the promenade by a dwarf wall. A pier, a switch-back, public gardens, and other places of amusements, have been built by the enterprise of the company, and in summer the town is thronged with excursionists from Yorkshire, Lancashire and the Midlands.*"

Admittedly the Official Album was blowing the company's own trumpet but did it not deserve to after what it had done for the area?

Before closing this chapter and moving into the 20th century it may well be worth taking a look at a scheme that failed. In the 1890's the Saltfleetby Light Railway was promoted to connect Grimsby and Mablethorpe via the coast. The planned route would have shared MS&L tracks until, east of New Clee station, it would swing away and

22. Grimsby, Union Dock, c.1935. Evidence of the rebuilding work at the Union Dock in the 1930's is visible here with extensive work being carried out around the original entrance to the Old Dock. What really catches the eye however is the multitude of both full and empty coal wagons in Brick Pit Sidings. The signal box of the same name is visible in the centre left of the view whilst Alexandra Dock signal box, already demolished, was to the right of the steam crane, adjacent to the curve in the new concrete walling.

Photo: H. L. Howe courtesy GLRPS

cross open country to Humberston. A branch would be built from there to a new station near Brighton Street in Cleethorpes. Here it was planned to join up with an extension of the present railway from Cleethorpes station. Immediately one sees that such a line would not only have severed Cleethorpes from its foreshore but strangled it in a triangle of railway lines. From Humberston the promoters planned to

continue south via North Cotes, Grainthorpe and South Somercotes to Saltfleetby, where the Great Northern branch to Mablethorpe came in from Louth. Instead of linking in with this line an independent route was planned into Mablethorpe and on to Sutton where it would have formed a junction with the GNR line from Mablethorpe to Willoughby. Needless to say the scheme was thrown out by a Parliamentary committee only to be revived in 1897, without the Grimsby and Cleethorpes sections. The revived line now planned to leave the East Lincolnshire line at New Waltham and join the original route at Humberston. A Light Railway Order was in fact granted by the Board of Trade in 1899 which included a branch from Humberston to Cleethorpes. Although the Great Northern Railway were interested in building the New Waltham – Saltfleetby section nothing came of it and the scheme quietly faded away. One can only be thankful that the lines around Cleethorpes were never built but, if the New Waltham – Saltfleetby section had materialised, would the coastal villages in between have developed in the same way that Cleethorpes and, to a lesser extent, Mablethorpe did? We shall never know.

23. Cleethorpes, 1960. The proximity of Cleethorpes station to the foreshore is evident in this aerial view taken in 1960. Suggitts Lane carriage sidings are alongside the big dipper with the turntable and signalbox, demolished in 1985, beyond. The six platform terminal station is at the top of the picture with the original station buildings on the right and the newer station buildings beyond the buffer stops. It is easy to see from this view how the planned extension to Brighton Street, out of view at the top of the picture, by the Saltfleetby Light Railway would have destroyed the seafront and left the foreshore marooned from the town. Cleethorpes Pier, possibly one of the shortest in the country, originally extended much further out into the river but it was destroyed by fire, rebuilt and eventually demolished in 1939 leaving only the part visible in the top right hand corner. The whole of the seafront from the Big Dipper to beyond the Pier was developed by the MS&LR. *Photo: Grimsby Evening Telegraph*

2 : Nemesis 1900-1934

In 1900 negotiations commenced between interested Grimsby parties and the Great Central Railway, the outcome of which was to be the jewel in the crown of the railway company, Immingham. Some would argue that the building of its main line to London in the 1890's is deserving of that honour but, surely, that is the crown itself.

Grimsby's docks in the 1890's were again being stretched to capacity with more space desparately needed. The Lancashire, Derbyshire and East Coast Railway was proposing a line from Warrington in Lancashire, to Sutton-on-Sea on the Lincolnshire coast, where it planned to build substantial dock installations. Although this would have eased the situation at Grimsby it would also have taken away trade from the town. By 1900 the threat of this dock ever being built was fast disappearing and to cover any possibility of it being revived one can only assume that the Grimsby business community made its overtures to the GCR.

There can be little doubt that the Great Central had been keeping a watchful eye on the LDECR and its plans for in 1901 they granted running powers, over its line from Lincoln to Grimsby, to the LDECR, thereby giving access to Grimsby docks to trains from the LDEC. In 1907 the LDECR became part of the Great Central Railway.

Ever conscious of the need to improve and expand its facilities at Grimsby, the GCR met favourably the proposals from the Grimsby businessmen. A new dock was sorely needed and the time had come to move away from the town so the GC revived in principal Liddell's plans of 1874. This conflicted with the views of the Grimsby people who wanted it built adjacent to the present docks but eventually the local people were won over, not so much by the persuasiveness of the railway company but because it was proved to be much cheaper to build a dock up river where the deep water channel ran close to the southern shore of the Humber. At Grimsby a dredged channel over a mile in length would be required to give ships access to the port whereas five miles or so upstream a channel only 300 yards long would be needed. Another factor was that the new port would be able to accept the largest ships of the day at any state of the tide, something that would never be possible at Grimsby so from a financial viewpoint the choice was obvious. A deep water channel is not only costly to create but with the swift flowing currents in the Humber is very costly to maintain. The price of land adjacent to Grimsby, which had become a large and thriving town, was at a premium whereas just a few miles away land was cheap. The people of Grimsby, after considering all this, accepted the proposal by the railway company and the seeds for a new dock at Immingham were sown.

The Great Central Railway, confident that their proposals would be accepted, acquired the land at Immingham from Lord Yarborough before the parties at Grimsby had made up their minds. The new dock was sanctioned by parliament under the title of the Humber Commercial Railway & Dock Act dated 22nd July 1904. The docks were to be built and owned by a nominally independent company and leased to the GCR for 999 years. However, the act of parliament left no doubt as to the responsibility of the Great Central in this venture.

On the 12th July 1906 there was a ceremony to honour the cutting of the first sod, this taking place about 100 yards from the shoreline and marked the commencement of the works. Guests were conveyed in special trains from Cleethorpes, London, Manchester and Chesterfield. Even though a tremendous thunderstorm, less than an hour before the guests arrived, did its best to destroy the marquees – in which a special luncheon was to be served – the day was destined to be a success. After a short service led by the Bishop of Lincoln, Lady Henderson, wife of the Chairman of the GCR, cut the first sod amidst loud applause and cheering. The luncheon over, several loyal toasts were proposed and the guests departed. The navvies and their equipment then moved in to complete a task which would occupy most of the next six years.

The dock estate when completed, covered over 1000 acres and its building employed nearly 3000 men, 30 locomotives, 1500 wagons, 10 steam navvies (excavators) and numerous cranes, pumps and pile drivers. There was over 100 miles of temporary railway track laid by the contractors. The company concerned was Price, Wills and Reeve and the total cost of the new installations was 2.6 million pounds, more than £900,000 of this being utilised in building the dock.

The whole of the area was very marshy and much of it was below the high water mark so the level of the land needed raising, this being done in two ways. Firstly, the earth removed from the dock area was used. Secondly, the deep water channel required a considerable amount of dredging and so the large quantities of mud removed from the river bed was pumped onto the land enabling the level of the land to be raised by about five feet. **continued on page 25**

24. Immingham Dock, 12th July 1906. Prescot, an 0-6-0ST belonging to the contractors, is seen here on 12th July 1906, the day Lady Henderson had the honour to cut the first sod. Prescot is in charge of the VIP train evidenced by the coach, which is the GCR directors saloon. Built at Gorton in 1890 this vehicle served successive owners for 78 years until, whilst working in the Scottish region, it was damaged beyond economical repair in an accident and scrapped.

Photo: Grimsby Public Libraries

25. Immingham, 1963. In this view rationalisation is already under way. Nos. 5, 6 and 7 coal hoists have been dismantled although it is possible to trace their positions from the scars left by the lifted tracks. The storage roads for the remaining four hoists can be seen with the return roads being positioned between, and shared by, Nos. 1 and 2 and Nos. 3 and 4 hoists, the last two being actively engaged in loading colliers. Both Empty and Reception Sidings are well filled with wagons although the northern part of Reception appears to be derelict. On the mineral quay the tracks that once joined one side of the quay to the other have also gone but as there is ample opportunity for crossing further along, this appears to have been an understandable economy measure. The course of the Humber Commercial Railway can be seen approaching Humber Road Junction in the top left corner of the photograph. The line to the East side of the dock can be seen running from this junction along the southern edge of Reception and Empty sidings, following the course of the yards before disappearing out of view in the bottom left hand corner and running past the loco sheds to Immingham East Junction. It is also possible to trace the line from Humber Road to Immingham West Junction which runs left to right just above the centre of the view. A diesel shunter with a number of wagons can just be made out heading along this line towards Humber Road. From the triangular West Junction the line to the Dock station is visible curving away to the right and out of view centre right. The Barton and Immingham is the thin black line running west from the junction and following the course of the river as far as the oil storage tanks in the distance. This is where Killingholme (Admiralty Platform) was located. Killingholme station is about half way between West Junction and the oil tanks whilst East Halton would have been situated just above the smoke from the burning stubble in the top left hand corner.

When reading the text it is difficult to imagine storage space for 17,000 wagons but one only has to consider the size of just one of the wagons that are visible and then take into account the fact that the major part of this photograph covers some of the yards, not all, that were available at Immingham.

Photo: Grimsby Evening Telegraph

26. Immingham, c.1920. The original station on the west side of Immingham Dock was Immingham Western Jetty. Situated further west than the later Immingham Dock station, its position can be fixed by noting the lines immediately behind the platform that are inclinded and are those leading to the girder bridges at Western Jetty. Also visible in this view above the primitive ticket office is the chimney of the power house.
Photo: Grimsby Public Libraries.

27. Immingham, Eastern Jetty, c.1924. Ex Great Northern Railway Ivatt Class C1 4-4-2 No. 1444 at the head of a boat train special at Eastern Jetty station, Immingham, circa 1924. It is waiting for passengers to disembark from the P&O liner alongside. Visits by such ships and, therefore, the need for such specials, ceased with the outbreak of war in 1939 and were, sadly, never revived. The jetty is now in use as an oil terminal.
Photo: Grimsby Public Libraries

2: continued from page 23

When complete the dock covered 45 acres and was basically rectangular in shape with a large quay 1,250 feet long by 350 feet wide extending into it on the western side. This quay dealt mainly with mineral traffic, iron and steel and there was a fixed crane of 50 tons capacity with ten smaller travelling cranes of 3 and 5 tons capacity. The northern arm of the dock formed by this quay became a huge timber pond which utilised 5 travelling steam cranes for the stacking of timber.

The whole of the southern quay was used for loading colliers through seven coal hoists, each capable of handling 700 tons of coal per hour. Each hoist, one of which was actually mobile to facilitate the faster loading of ships when necessary, was served by eight gravity fed sidings which could hold 320 loaded wagons.

The eastern quays and the remaining part of the northern quay, extending eastwards from the lock gates, were covered by three huge transit sheds with a total length of 900 feet and a width of 140 feet. No. 1 transit shed was on the northern quay whilst Nos. 2 and 3 were on the eastern quay. They were serviced internally by 9 jib cranes and externally by 14 cranes of 10 and 12 tons capacity. Immediately behind Nos. 2 and 3 transit sheds a huge granary was built. Original plans envisaged the eastern side of the dock to be a mirror image of the western side and this would have made the dock almost twice its present size and appearing similar to a letter H laid on its side. This part of the plan was abandoned around the time construction commenced.

The dock was entered through a lock pit 840 feet long and alongside the western edge was a 740 feet long graving dock. In the river were two jetties commencing at the entrance to the lock pit and extending, at a slight outward angle, into the river before swinging east and west respectively. The eastern jetty was provided with a landing stage for passengers and was served, initially, by a double track railway which terminated at a station on the jetty. The western jetty was built primarily for bunkering the large amount of coal fired ships then plying the oceans. Wagons were propelled by locomotives over a girder bridge out to a coal hoist on the jetty and empty wagons returned by gravity over a second girder bridge. This jetty was the first part of the new docks to be used when, on 17th June 1910, the Great central steamer *Dewsbury* availed itself of the facilities.

To provide all the power needed for the dock estate a power house was erected close to the girder bridges of the western jetty. This power house contained 9 Lancashire boilers and four 630 h.p. engines. The boiler house also provided electric current for the Grimsby – Immingham tramway (q.v.). The whole of the dock complex was presided over by, and administered from, the dock offices which were built on the eastern side of the lock pits.

Being built in the days before mass road transport a venture of this kind required massive rail installations, therefore storage space for nearly 17,000 wagons was provided in sidings which in total measured

continued on page 28

DOCKS AND INLAND WATERWAYS EXECUTIVE.
(HUMBER PORTS)
IMMINGHAM DOCK.

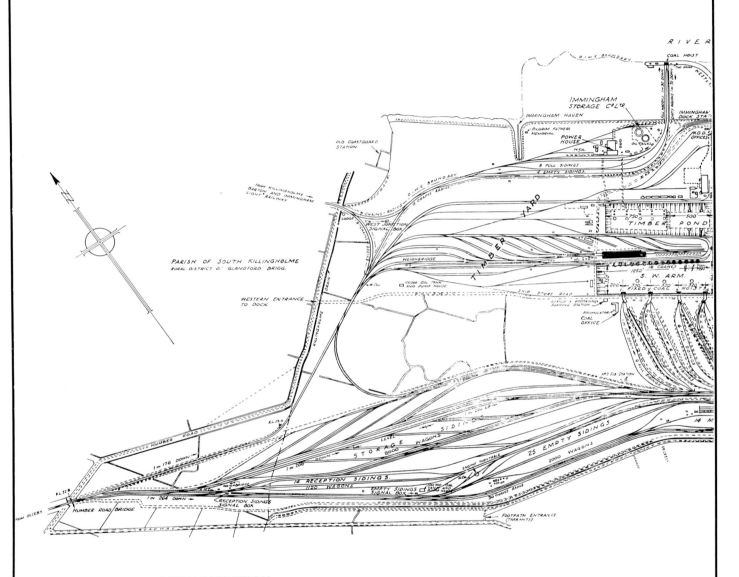

ACCOMMODATION

Water area - - - - - - - - - - - - -	45 acres
Length of quays and berthage - - - - - - - - -	9097 feet
Width of entrance - - - - - - - - - - -	90 feet
Length of lock - - - - - - - - - - - -	840 feet
Total length of railway track in and about the dock - - - -	166 miles
Graving Dock - - - - - - - - - - - -	length 740 feet

Depth of Water on Sill M.H.W.S. 47 ft. 11 in.

Depth of Water on Sill M.H.W.N. 43 ft. 3 in.

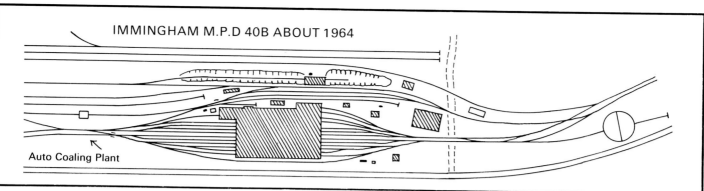

IMMINGHAM M.P.D 40B ABOUT 1964

Auto Coaling Plant

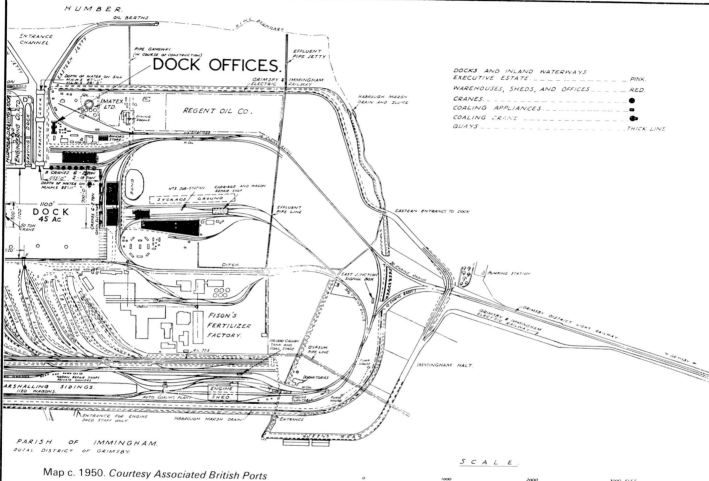

DOCK OFFICES.

Map c. 1950. *Courtesy Associated British Ports*

DOCKS AND INLAND WATERWAYS	
EXECUTIVE ESTATE	PINK.
WAREHOUSES, SHEDS, AND OFFICES	RED.
CRANES.	
COALING APPLIANCES.	
COALING CRANE	
QUAYS	THICK LINE

SCALE.

PARISH OF IMMINGHAM.
RURAL DISTRICT OF GRIMSBY.

EQUIPMENT

Two deep water jetties east and west of entrance

Six hydraulic coal hoists - - - - - - capacity 700 tons per hour each

Siding capacity for 174,000 tons of coal

Timber pond - - - - - - - - - - - - area 6 acres

Mineral quay with seventeen 3- to 50-ton hydraulic cranes *

Grain warehouse - - - - - - - - - capacity 15,000 tons

Two movable grain elevators - - - - capacity 100 150 tons per hour

Wool warehouse - - - - - - - - - - capacity 40,000 bales

Bonded store with covered floor - - - - - area 7,192 sq. ft.

Four transit sheds and warehouses - - - - Covered floor area 173,500 sq. ft.
(equipped with cranes and hoists)

Fourteen hydraulic luffing cranes on Nos. One and Two Quays - capacity 2-10 tons

Passenger platform on eastern jetty

* Iron ore grabs fitted to 5-ton cranes

2: continued from page 25

some 170 miles in length. To service the large fleet of locomotives required to operate in the docks and to haul the large amount of goods traffic generated by the port a 12 road locomotive depot, complete with repair facilities, was built in the south east corner of the dock estate. A large coaling stage was built along the northern side of the shed, a mechanical coaling plant being added at the western end of the depot in the 1930's. Two turntables were installed, both measuring 65 feet, one at the eastern end of the depot and the other at the eastern end of the reception sidings. A dormitory block was built a few years after the depot alongside the depot turntable. This was a necessity for crews from other depots who booked off duty after bringing a train into Immingham and needed somewhere to stay until their next shift. The depot, suffering like Grimsby from supplies of hard water, was provided with a water softening plant in 1915.

With the opening of the depot at Immingham the engine shed at Grimsby diminished in importance, even to the extent that Immingham supplied the passenger engines for the services out of Cleethorpes. Whether the GCR originally intended to build such a large depot at Immingham is questionable. Cleveland Bridge, better known to

generations of Grimsby people as the "Tip", was constructed to carry Gilbey Road over the new railway at Little Coates on the western side of Grimsby. Two large openings, crossed by girder bridges, remained, one providing access from the new Great Coates branch to the docks and the other, according to rumour, was for access to a new locomotive depot. A depot, built alongside West Marsh siding would seem to be a logical move for the depot in Railway Street would not be large enough to cope with all the new work and therefore a centrally placed depot would become a necessity. A new depot would need to be readily accessible by locomotives from several different directions so at Cleveland Bridge the depot would be close to the yards at the Alexandra Dock, no more than five miles from Immingham and about two or three miles, by rail, from the east side of Grimsby and Cleethorpes. Did the Great Central originally plan to build its new depot at Cleveland bridge or not? It is doubtful if we shall ever know.

As already stated, the first ship left the western jetty in June 1910 although the official opening was not scheduled to take place for another two years. The date selected was Monday 22nd July 1912 and the ceremony was to be performed by His Majesty King George V.

28. Immingham, East Junction, 24th May 1961. Arrangements for road traffic to cross the Grimsby and Immingham Light Railway were similar at both ends of the line. At Grimsby, Gilbey Road crossed the railway via Cleveland bridge and at Immingham, Queens Road crossed the railway in a similar fashion. In this view of the bridge at Immingham part of the triangular East junction is visible beneath the left hand arch with the cranes alongside nos. 2 and 3 transit sheds in the distance. In recent years the right hand fork of the junction has been lifted. GCR car No. 16 is crossing the bridge on a service to Grimsby. *Photo: J. H. Price*

29. Immingham, c.1958. When Immingham Dock was built, Immingham was still a small village some distance away. The large loco shed, built on the dock estate, was required to service not only its own allocation of locomotives but many from other depots on the GCR system. These visiting locos also brought with them crews who needed rest and relaxation after a hard days work. Immingham was too small and Grimsby considered too far away, therefore, the GCR built a dormitory block adjacent to the north east corner of the depot. Known by locomen as the "Barracks" it is seen here in the late 1950's. *Photo: R. Dane*

Special trains ran from London and Manchester. Local people were carried over the Grimsby District Railway (q.v.) and the tramway in trains packed to capacity, additional services supplementing those scheduled. Other trains brought more visitors to Grimsby from Hull, via the ferry and New Holland, and Cleethorpes.

The Great Northern Royal train arrived at Grimsby Town station at 12.45 p.m. where the King and Queen Mary were received by the Chairman of the Great Central Railway, Sir Alexander Henderson, and its General manager, Sam Fay, the High Steward of Grimsby, Lord Heneage, the local M.P., Sir George Doughty, and A. J. Knott J.P., the Mayor. After meeting members of the Corporation the King and Queen left in carriages for Grimsby Docks station. The Royal train, hauled by No. 364 *Lady Henderson*, one of J. G. Robinsons magnificent compound Atlantics, departed at 1.30 p.m., and the train arrived at a specially constructed platform opposite the lock pits at Immingham 50 minutes later. Boarding the paddle steamer *Killingholme*, their Majesties travelled through the lock pits and made a circuit of the docks before alighting alongside No. 2 transit shed. After several presentations and a short service the chairman of the GCR gave a short speech during which he requested permission for the new dock to be called the King's Dock.

The King, after declaring the dock open, granted permission for it to be known by its new name, a name which few people realise ever existed. Then, to the surprise of everyone but Sir Alexander Henderson, Sam Fay was summoned to the dais and, in front of the assembled multitude, was asked to kneel whereupon the King bestowed upon him a knighthood. It is said that, so popular was this act and, so loudly did the crowd cheer, the applause was heard in Grimsby. This final act brought to a close a great day in the annals of the Great Central Railway. Immingham, the worlds newest deep water port, was officially open for business.

In the days when Immingham Dock was built the railways were the lifeblood of the country and without a rail link the new dock could never hope to flourish. The closest the railway came to Immingham

before the dock was planned had been at Little London between Stallingborough and Habrough. Isolated from the rail network, therefore, Immingham was in desperate need of a rail link and subsequently, it was in fact, to get three.

Part of the new rail network required the realignment of the Great Coates branch. From a triangular junction, known as Marsh Junction, the branch now turned north for just under a mile before swinging east into the dock estate. The original Great Coates branch closed around 1908.

The first of the new lines connected Immingham with Grimsby and was planned as part of the Grimsby District Light Railway. Completed in May 1906 this line left the Great Coates branch near Pyewipe Road and, never more than half a mile from the river, ran north westwards for five and three quarter miles to Immingham. Towards the end of 1909 public pressure forced the GCR to run a passenger service along the branch for the growing workforce at Immingham as, until that time it had been in the exclusive hands of the contractors. Small wooden platforms were built at either end, the one at Grimsby being known as Pyewipe Road and the other as Immingham Halt.

The second of the new lines was the Humber Commercial Railway which connected Immingham with the Grimsby – New Holland line just to the north of Ulceby station. From this point the line ran eastwards to Humber Road Junction (3½ miles) where it diverged, one set of tracks running along the south side of the dock estate providing access to the coal hoists and marshalling yards. It then carried on past the locomotive depot to join the Grimsby District Light Railway at the triangular Immingham East Junction. From here the line swung north and then west to run alongside the river before heading north again onto the Eastern Jetty. The other set of tracks carried on northwards from Humber Road Junction and then east, providing access to the Western jetty, and terminating at Immingham Dock station. Although far from complete the line opened on 3rd January 1910, probably for the use of the contractors as the first coal train did not use it for another six months. However, it was not fully completed until May 1912 when,

30. Grimsby Town, 22nd July 1912. Mr. Tom Jervis (seated on left) the Grimsby Town station master, poses proudly on a garlanded platform 2 with some of the extra police drafted in for the visit of King George V, on the day the King officially opened Immingham Dock. Mr. Jervis' two daughters are the young ladies stood amongst the constables on the left and his son is the young man third from right. *Photo: Mrs. Baker*

31. (Above) Grimsby, West Marsh, c.1970.
West Marsh Sidings as seen from Cleveland Bridge. The through lines, i.e. the second Great Coates branch, are third and fourth from the left. In the background, just discernable, is Marsh Junction signal box with the main line into Grimsby running past it from right to left. There are still a good number of wagons in the sidings, which require the attention of two pilots, although the coal wagons appear to be some ex GWR vehicles purchased by Peter Dixons around that time to replace the ageing Dock Use Only vehicles used for transporting wood pulp from the docks to the mill.
Photo: Grimsby Public Libraries

32. (Left) East Halton, 24th September 1962.
The Barton and Immingham Light Railway was built as single track but, as can be seen in this view of East Halton, sufficient land being purchased should traffic require the line to be doubled, something which proved unnecessary. This view shows the basic facilities provided for passengers and the lack of even a siding for goods traffic.
Photo: D. Thompson

double track throughout, it measured a total length of 8¼ miles.

The third new line was the Barton and Immingham Light Railway. As the name suggests the original plan envisaged a line from Barton to Immingham which would cross the Grimsby to New Holland line just south of Goxhill station. However, by the time the line was built there had been some tightening of the purse strings and only the section from Goxhill to Immingham was constructed. From a junction ½ mile south of Goxhill station the line ran eastwards until it met, by means of a triangular junction, the Humber Commercial Railway at Immingham West Junction, a distance of just over 7 miles. The first part of the line, Immingham West to Killingholme, opened at the beginning of December 1910 with the remaining section opening six months later. There were two stations on the line, East Halton and Killingholme, both opening on 2nd May 1911. A third station, Killingholme Admiralty Platform, followed later.

The three new railways gave Immingham its access to the outside world. The most important of these has alway been the Humber Commercial Railway which, via the Ulceby – Brocklesby curve, brought in goods from the rest of the GCR system. The Barton and Immingham gave access to Hull via the ferry, although this was really limited to people rather than goods whilst the Grimsby District provided room for transfer freights between the various docks in the area as well as for light engine movements between Immingham and Grimsby. The Great Central held Immingham secure in its bosom, its closest competitor, the Great Northern, at Grimsby, was now more of an ally. In fact, whilst Immingham was being built, these two

companies, together with the Great Eastern Railway, agreed to amalgamate, although fearing a monopoly, parliament threw out the idea.

There was however, plans to build a fourth railway. The Lancashire and Yorkshire Railway, in the early years of the 20th century, was continuously looking for ways to gain access to North Lincolnshire. Already it had gained access to the Isle of Axholme via the Isle of Axholme Light Railway although there can be little doubt, however, that its real goal was the east coast ports of Immingham and Grimsby and the lucrative traffic that they generated. In 1904 it was instrumental in proposing the Ackworth and Lindsey Light Railway. This line would have crossed the Isle of Axholme and tunnelled under the Trent and then proceeded via Barton, Goxhill and East Halton to a junction with the Humber Commercial Railway. This proposal was easily defeated by the Great Central and the North Eastern Railway, who were originally involved in the scheme but realised that through it they would lose a considerable amount of trade which passed along its own lines to the docks at Hull.

The large increase in railborne traffic that would be generated when Immingham opened also necessitated improvements to the permanent way elsewhere in the area, principally between Wrawby Junction and

Brocklesby so in 1912 the GCR let a contract for £40,000 to C. J. Willis and Sons for the quadrupling of the track along this section and to G. A. Pillatt, for £9,113, for the reconstruction of Barnetby station. Mackenzie and Holland supplied the signalling equipment at a cost of £16,538, this figure presumably including the reconstruction of Wrawby Junction, Barnetby East and Brocklesby Junction signal boxes and the construction of Barnetby West box. The last mentioned, along with a small signal box controlling the lime sidings at Melton Ross, have since been demolished. At Barnetby the original station had consisted of a single platform, on which stood the station buildings, for Grimsby bound trains, and an island platform catering for trains travelling in the opposite direction. The new layout provided two island platforms, one each for trains in either direction, connected to the station buildings by a footbridge. The station layout at Brocklesby remained virtually unaltered with the new lines looping around the outside of the station and the down platform becoming an island. The level crossing at the west end of the station however, was replaced by a road overbridge, the completed scheme being brought into use in 1915. The up relief line left the main line east of Brocklesby station and bypassed it alongside the station buildings within feet of the front door of the station masters house, a curious practice which must have given the unknowing visitor a few frights on opening the door to find a large steam engine literally on top of him. An unusual aspect of the rebuilding, for the GCR, was the siting of the signalbox on the island platform.

Two years after the official opening of Immingham the country was at war. The new port, as well as Grimsby, was to play a considerable part during hostilities, both being taken over by the Royal Navy. The Great Centrals' fleet of steamships were also called up all except three, the *Bury, City of Leeds* and *City of Bradford*, which were unfortunate in being caught in German territorial waters before they could effect an escape, and were seized. The railways and docks during the war period were stretched to capacity supplying coal for bunkering the hundreds of coal fired ships operated by the Navy. As a result, over 3,000 loaded coal wagons were held in the dock area at Immingham and often as many as nine coal trains each day made their way from South Wales to the port. From August 1914 to March 1919 Immingham handled 1,930 coal trains specifically for the Navy.

During this period of expansion at Immingham the Great Central suffered losses at both Grimsby and Cleethorpes due to fire. In 1903 the most impressive part of the sea front at Cleethorpes, the Pier pavilion, was totally destroyed by fire on 29th June, followed a month later by No. 10 grain warehouse at Grimsby, which also went up in flames. A little over ten years later, on 26th June 1914, a warehouse and a bonded store were destroyed in a similar fashion.

From midnight on 31st December 1922 the Great Central Railway, benefactor of so much in the Grimsby area, ceased to exist. The grouping of the railways from the 1st January 1923 saw the GCR amalgamate with the Great Northern Railway, the Great Eastern Railway, the North Eastern Railway, the North British Railway, the Great North of Scotland Railway and several smaller companies to form the London and North Eastern Railway. For over seventy years the Great Central and its predecessor, the Manchester, Sheffield and Lincolnshire had nurtured and developed the area and although of importance to the LNER, the Grimsby area was now a smaller cog in a much larger wheel. The area still repaid its investment and attracted additional capital to extend the fish docks.

Whilst Immingham was under construction the GCR did not forget Grimsby, more than £150,000 being spent on improvements to the docks. Such was the state of the fishing industry, however, that the fish docks were in danger of being choked by the number of vessels using the port. The tonnage of fish landed had expanded from just over 71,000 tons in 1891 to just under 180,000 tons in 1910, almost all the fish leaving Grimsby by rail whilst the coal for the trawlers came in by the same means. It was, therefore, in the railways interests to provide sufficient space and facilities for the trawling fleet. Negotiations between the GCR and the fishing vessel owners opened in August 1911 followed seven months later by a meeting with other interested parties. By the end of 1912 the necessary Act of Parliament had been passed and the Great Central were committed to an outlay of around £500,000 to construct a new fish dock with new lock pits, widen the link between Nos. 1 and 2 Fish Dock and to install new sidings at New Clee. Before the new works could be implemented World War I intervened and the project was shelved.

The plan, destined to be the last major improvement by a railway company in the area, was not revived until the 1930's when the LNER, in collaboration with Grimsby Corporation, undertook to construct the dock first mooted in 1912, though the cost by now had risen to £1.7 million. The new dock, No. 3 Fish Dock, covered 38 acres and was a continuation eastwards of the original, No. 1, fish dock. In the new dock, the North Wall, 1,985 feet long and built as part of an embankment 7,500 ft long to seal off the new dock from the river during construction, was reserved for trawlers preparing for sea. Along the South Quay, slipways, capable of handling ships up to 1,080 tons, were built for repairing the ships together with two quays extending into the dock where refitting could be completed. These quays were 397 ft long and 266 ft long respectively, one having a 5 ton travelling crane and the other a similar one of 15 tons. On the eastern side of the dock three coal hoists were installed for bunkering the trawlers and extensive sidings extended from these, almost to Fuller Street in Cleethorpes, for the storage of coal wagons. The official opening of No. 3 Fish Dock took place on 4th October 1934.

Finally, in 1914 the problems caused by the GNR level crossing at Weelsby Road came under discussion. Proposals were made to replace it with a subway but once again, World War I halted these plans. In 1919 the problem was again discussed but it was not until May 1933 that an improvement scheme was finally started. Costing £20,000 and contracted to Fletcher & Co. of Mansfield the level crossing was to be replaced by the present 200 ton plate girder bridge under which was constructed a subway. Completion, including demolition of the gate-house, was scheduled for January 1934 but was actually sufficiently complete to allow the Mayor of Grimsby to open it in early December 1933. He did this by being driven under it in a double decker bus.

33. Weelsby Road, c.1910. Travelling along Weelsby Road today, it is difficult to imagine in the hustle and bustle of traffic that where now there stands a subway there was once a quiet, almost rural, level crossing. This view shows Weelsby Road before the subway and possibly, judging by the dress of the woman opposite the crossing keepers house, before the First World War. The newly built houses in the distance are in Hainton Avenue and beyond them is Weelsby Woods.
Photo: Welholme Galleries

34. Grimsby, c.1952. The Fish Docks as seen from the air in the early 1950's. The original, No. 1 Fish Dock, is in the top right hand corner and No. 2 Fish Dock is in the top left. Access to No. 2 Fish Dock was through a narrow channel in the centre of the picture and trawlers passing through this channel were controlled by traffic lights. A small swing bridge at this point gave access to the Pontoon from the east side of the dock. Beyond these, stretching across the top of the picture, is the Royal Dock. In the foreground is No. 3 Fish Dock with its three, sentinel like, coal shutes. Typical representatives of Grimsby's then large deep water trawling fleet can be seen moored in both No. 2 and No. 3 Fish Docks whilst a group of the smaller seine netters are huddled together in the top right corner of No. 1 Fish Dock. The smoke from two steam locos shunting the Pontoon in Murray Street can be seen on the extreme left.

In the foreground both full and empty coal wagons, along with numerous fish vans stand in the sidings built to serve the coal hoists whilst to the left the scars left by lifted sidings are rapidly healing. Today it is impossible to identify this area as once being railway property as cold stores and the Ross Young's factory complex now cover the site.

Photo: E. Green

3 : Decline — from 1935 onwards

The docks and railways worked efficiently during the inter war years, although the docks did not survive unscathed from the misery of World War I and the depression, coal exports suffering in particular. As happened during the First World War the docks were requisitioned on the outbreak of the 1939 conflict. Once again both docks and railways excelled themselves with the service they gave to the nation. The twenties and thirties, however halcyon they may have seemed, witnessed the development of something that was to grow and progressively attack, the very lifeblood of the railway system, its ability to carry goods and passengers more quickly than any other form of transport. This destructive monster was, of course, the efficient and economical road vehicle.

The first closure in the area has already been noted in the previous chapter, that of the original Great Coates branch. The next closures came towards the end of 1939 when, as a wartime economy measure, the halts at Weelsby Road and Grainsby were closed, happily to be reopened on the cessation of hostilities. Around the same date Immingham Eastern Jetty, which had seen the embarkation of so many passengers on to cruise liners in the 1920's and 1930's, closed. This station, like so many to follow, was doomed never to reopen although the jetty itself survives and is now used as an oil terminal. In 1941, as recorded elsewhere, New Holland loco depot ceased to be an independent entity and lived out its final years as a sub-shed of Immingham. In April of the same year Riby Street Platforms also closed. As this is the last time that this small halt will be mentioned perhaps it would be appropriate to give it the title by which the majority of locals knew it, namely Skate Nob Junction.

The closures listed above were the only ones carried out by the LNER, but before it ceased to exist as a separate entity, however, it did sanction the doubling of the track along the Grimsby District Light Railway and this was carried out during 1948 under the auspices of British Railways. This was not the curtain raiser to a new series of railway developments for the area however, as decline and closure more and more became the norm. The light railway was singled again in 1984.

The post war LNER new works programme included a provision of £500,000 for improvements to Cleethorpes station (qv) and £1,300,000 for a new station in the East Marsh, to replace both Town and Docks stations, and also for a new goods and coal depot to replace the ones demolished to make way for the new passenger station. As has always happened with plans for a central station in the East Marsh no action was ever taken.

The axe fell first on the two halts temporarily closed during the war, Weelsby Road and Grainsby. They survived for just seven years after reopening, finally closing on the 10th March 1952. Holton Le Clay lost its passenger service on the 4th July 1955, followed six years later on the 11th September 1961 by Fotherby, Utterby, Ludborough (passengers only), Holton Village, Waltham (passengers only), and Hainton Street. Goods facilities were withdrawn from Ludborough and Holton Le Clay on 25th May 1964 followed by Waltham on the 15th June. North Thoresby, the only one of the East Lincs. line stations not mentioned so far, closed to goods traffic on the 30th December 1963 but maintained a passenger service until the 5th October 1970.

As with many other parts of the rail network it was the Beeching report of 1963 that sealed the fate of the East Lincs. line. The report favoured closure of the whole line between Garden Street Junction, Grimsby and Werrington Junction, Peterborough together with the closure of the New Holland – Barton branch and the cessation of passenger services between Cleethorpes and New Holland. This latter

35. Hainton Street Halt, August 1961. The halt, which is in Welholme Road, is named after Hainton Street, later Hainton Avenue, which runs parallel to the east side of the line. The halts on the East Lincs line were opened in 1905 and were served by the Grimsby–Louth motor trains. The coaches used on these trains had specially fitted steps to gain access to the low platforms but when they were replaced by DMU's, individual steps were kept on the platforms. Hainton Street is the only surviving signal box on the East Lincs line between Louth North and Garden Street.

Photo: B. Clark courtesy Grimsby Public Libraries

36. Holton Village Halt, 19th August 1961. Holton Village Halt looking south. Of a more substantial construction than the other halts along the line it was much closer to the village of Holton le Clay than the station of that name, in fact the village has now expanded to cover the fields on both sides of the line in this view and makes one think that if only the East Lincs had stayed open this small halt could now be a vital link for people living in the village and working in Grimsby. A total of eight trains from Grimsby called at the halt during the week although one (the 3.2 pm ex Grimsby) was conditional on Fridays only.   *Photo: D. Thompson*

would almost certainly have lead to the closure of the New Holland line north of Ulceby. However, the Barton branch and, therefore, the New Holland line have remained open to this day. Not so the East Lincs. for after a tremendous fight by the people living along the line to keep it open closure came on the 5th October 1970. The section between Grimsby and Louth survived as a freight only branch for a further ten years, closing finally in December 1980.

Some twelve years after the closure of the line south of Louth, British Rail issued a temporary amendment to the working timetables. This stated that, in the event of the temporary closure of the Lincoln to Barnetby line, trains should be routed from Lincoln via Louth and the East Lincs. line. Just how these trains were to traverse the trackless wastes of East Lincolnshire was not explained and one can only hope that this error has since been amended as there is no one left at Louth, in railway service, who would be able to oblige the driver of a block oil train whistling for the road at Wragby Junction.

The next line in the area to close, and so far the last, was the Barton and Immingham Light Railway. Passenger services were withdrawn on the 17th June 1963, occasioning the closure of the stations at Killingholme, Killingholme (Admiralty Platform) and East Halton. Goods facilities were maintained at Killingholme until 4th January 1965. The Immingham end of this line still survives, providing important links to the various oil refineries and private sidings in the area. It is possible that, in the next few years, a new power station will be

built at Killingholme and if so, this line, whose trackbed is apparently still owned by British Rail, may re-open for the use of merry-go-round coal trains. It must be pointed out however that this is only speculation. Immingham Dock, or Western Jetty station maintained a passenger service for dock workers until 8th October 1969, when services via the Humber Commercial Railway and Ulceby to Grimsby ceased.

The stations at New Holland Town and Pier had been living on borrowed time since 1967, which was when the go ahead was given for building the Humber Bridge. It was apparent that as soon as the bridge opened there would be no further need for the ferry service. Goods facilities were withdrawn on the 3rd November 1979 at New Holland Town and two days later at the Pier. This would have been when the last of the coal fired paddle steamers, *Lincoln Castle*, was retired. Closure to passengers came on the 24th June 1981 on the day the bridge opened, a way of life gone forever. Barton now became the terminus of the passenger service from Cleethorpes with trains gaining access to the Barton branch via the south curve of the triangle at New Holland. It was on this curve that a new halt of timber construction was built for passengers living in or visiting New Holland. One must point out that, although by no means as attractive as the original Town station the new halt is much closer and, therefore, more convenient to the village.

With the exception of the two at New Holland, mentioned above, all of the stations remain open between Cleethorpes and Barton, as does Brocklesby and Barnetby which are situated to the west of this line. All

37. North Thoresby, 19th August 1961. North Thoresby station looking south on a wet and windy day. North Thoresby took its place in table 54 of the passenger services timetable for the Eastern Region (Sept-June 1957-58). During weekdays a dozen or so trains stopped for passengers heading in the Grimsby direction, the first two, apart from a Mondays only to set down, being local workings from Louth. In the Peterborough direction fewer trains called but the Louth workings balanced. Passenger services, withdrawn on 5th October 1970, outlived goods facilities which had ended some seven years earlier on 30th December 1963.

Photo: D. Thompson

38. Killingholme (Admiralty Platform), 27th September 1962. Killingholme (Admiralty Platform) was a later addition to the Barton & Immingham and opened in connection with a nearby naval seaplane base. This station was possibly unique in that it rarely, if ever, appeared in timetables but remained in regular use until the closure of the line. The view, taken from a passing train, also shows evidence of nearby Immingham's increasing use as an oil terminal.

Photo: D. Thompson

39. Thornton Abbey, n.d. This station opened 15 months after the opening of the line and replaced a temporary structure half a mile away named after the nearest village, Thornton Curtis. The station buildings were on the down platform and the station is, more or less, equidistant between Thornton Curtis and East Halton. Although East Halton acquired its own station on the Barton and Immingham in May 1911 it was still more convenient for the villagers to use Thornton Abbey when travelling to Grimsby as the service was more frequent. *Photo: G. Biddle*

the village stations lost their goods facilities around 1964. However, Cleethorpes station buildings were extensively modernised in 1961 and the track layout remodelled in 1985, when the number of available platforms was reduced from six to five. The station buildings at both New Clee and Grimsby Docks have been demolished, passengers at New Clee having to stand in the open no matter what the weather may be like. At least a crumb of comfort has been thrown to those waiting for trains at Grimsby Docks where a bus type shelter has been constructed. There has been little visual change at Grimsby Town over the years although the roof was replaced during June and July 1978 and the bay at the east end of Platform 1 is now used for car parking. The relief lines around the outside of the station have been lifted and the track layout simplified. Great Coates, Healing and Stallingborough all retain their main station buildings although now in private hands, passenger facilities being catered for with basic shelters on each platform. Habrough is probably the least changed of any of the local stations, all of its buildings still standing and in railway use with a complement of railway staff. This is due to its elevation to the rank of an Inter City station it being the closest to the docks at Immingham, all passenger trains stopping at Habrough.

Brocklesby, visually, is little changed although, again, its buildings have passed into private hands. Ulceby is now a single wooden platform raised about 2 feet higher than the old stone platform, which survives beneath it. This is the former Grimsby bound platform and cover is provided by the usual utilitarian shelter, all traces of the station buildings having been removed as has the other platform. Thornton Abbey still retains both platforms and these appear to both be still in use although the station buildings have gone in favour of the basic shelter. Somewhat strangely, this station has retained its LNER nameboards. Goxhill still retains all of its station buildings although those on the New Holland platform are derelict and the station house is in private hands. Barrow Haven, never sumptuous, is now just a small platform with the ubiquitous bus shelter. Ulceby, Thornton Abbey and Barrow Haven are request stops only, i.e. if you are travelling on the train you must inform the guard of your desire to alight at one of these stations, conversely if you wish to board a train at one of these stations you must put out your hand to signal the train to stop. Barton, which is now the terminus of the line, greets potential customers with a bus shelter, its buildings having been demolished.

Since 1948, although Immingham has seen a great reduction in railborne goods trains, this has been countered by an increase in block oil and iron ore trains. The subsequent reduction in the number of yards required for wagons is almost nothing when compared with the devastation that has swept over Grimsby. The vast network of sidings at New Clee which once held wagons full of coal for the trawling fleet and excursion trains from Cleethorpes, or witnessed the assembling of countless fish trains, have not been reduced, they have been obliterated, nothing remaining. At Fish Dock Road, where the various lines serving the Pontoon in the Fish Docks once came together to form more sidings for the assembling of fish trains and where, alongside, lines served the east side of the Royal Dock there is nothing. The connection to the west side of the Royal Dock over the swing bridge at Union Dock and the

40. New Clee, 29th May 1957. The sidings at New Clee were extensive and ran alongside the main line from New Clee station as far as Fuller Street and covered most of the land between the railway and the Humber bank. They were built to handle fish trains and incoming coal traffic as well as a holding area for excursions visiting Cleethorpes.

Visible in the distance of this view from Fuller Street footbridge are the Dock Tower and the three coal hoists in No. 3 Fish Dock. The sidings are full and a J94 is busy marshalling fish vans. Ten years later these same sidings would be virtually empty and redundant. The state of the track on the extreme right is of interest and it is assumed that it was laid shortly before World War II for transporting materials for a new sea wall, built from concrete blocks, and had been unused since. The angle of the track shows the affect that a storm can have and was probably damaged during the East Coast floods of 1953.

Photo: J. H. Meredith

sidings along the south side of the Union Dock are now but a memory. The disappearance of coal burning trawlers and the decline of Grimsby as a fishing port are contributory factors to the decline of these facilities and they must be considered, along with the transfer of the remaining fish traffic to road transport, as the reasons for the closures at New Clee and on the Fish Docks.

Ironically after many years of desperate need for some form of bridge over the railway at Cleethorpe Road one was built in 1967 and to build it the Royal Hotel had to be demolished. Still, no more would road traffic have to wait whilst goods and fish trains began their journey westwards or arrived home to be refilled with fish or empty their goods for export. No more would road traffic be delayed as the endless procession of excursions wound their way around the tortuous curves past the Fish Docks. No more would road traffic be delayed by the various passenger trains running into and out of Cleethorpes. No more. The fish trains were withdrawn almost simultaneously with the opening of the flyover. Goods trains disappeared too, whilst the number of excursions rolling into Cleethorpes were reduced to such a level that if one arrives today it is quite an event. The passenger service remains and is probably frequent enough to justify the building of the flyover but it really came sixty years too late.

Sidings still remain at East Marsh although drastically reduced in number and, seemingly, left to quietly rust away in the hope that one day they might once again become shiny with the continuous movement of goods trains. The goods sheds at Newmarket Street are closed, one having been demolished, with the coal depot at Holles Street sharing the same fate. This came in 1984, just a few years after the announcement that Holles Street was to become the coal concentration depot for the area. There was also a plan to build a liner terminal in the area but nothing came of it. The GN Goods at Pasture Street is now the site of two large retail stores, the goods shed having been demolished in 1978, and there are plans to build a new link road from this site along the trackbed of the old East Lincs. line as far as Waltham.

At West Marsh use is still made of the remaining sidings but once again the number is greatly reduced. Great Coates Sidings, adjacent to the western end of the Alexandra Dock have disappeared completely whilst the timber sidings along the south side of the same dock now carry a completely different type of traffic. Road traffic. The A180 trunk road has been built over this section. North of the Alexandra Dock about half of the Brick Pit Sidings remain in use although the timber yards to the east of these are now but a memory. A few sidings remain on the west side of the Royal Dock but, once again, they are much reduced in number.

The tremendous reduction in the goods and fish trains using the east side of the Royal Dock and the excursions visiting Cleethorpes, recorded earlier in this chapter, justified British Rail in looking closely at the future of the Cleethorpes branch. The outlook was gloomy with complete closure being one of the options. The eventual outcome however was not to be closure but to make the line single track. This took place in 1985, at a cost of £1.2 million, and is in operation from west of Pasture Street to Cleethorpes.

As far as the locomotive depots are concerned the decline and closure of both Grimsby and New Holland have already been recorded. Immingham though, has survived. A new diesel depot was built in 1966 to the east of the steam shed. Immingham closed to steam traction early in 1966. To facilitate the construction of the diesel depot half of the steam shed was demolished, the remaining half being used as a wagon repair shop. Today it is quite easy to imagine Immingham shed as it used to be in steam days as not only half of the steam shed survived but both the coaling tower and the coaling stage still stand, mute reminders of the past.

Signal boxes were once a common feature of the railway scene, but daily they grow fewer. Although not all in use at the same time there follows a list of all the known boxes within the current boundaries of Grimsby and Cleethorpes followed by a list of those still in use in 1987.

Cleethorpes, Suggitts Lane, New Clee, Fish Dock Road, Cleethorpe Road, New Bridge, Holme Street, Pasture Street (original), Pasture Street (1961), Goods Junction, Hainton Street, Weelsby Road, Garden Street, Wellowgate, Friargate Crossing, Littlefield Crossing, Marsh Junction, Great Coates, Great Coates Sidings No. 1, Great Coates Sidings No. 2, West Marsh Junction, Brick Pit Sidings, Alexandra Dock, Union Dock, Pyewipe Road, Macauley Lane. Total 26.

Pasture Street (1961), Hainton Street (out of use, line closed), Garden Street, Wellowgate, Friargate Crossing, Littlefield Crossing, Marsh Junction, Great Coates Sidings No. 1, Pyewipe Road. Total 9.

Of the nine that remain it is only a matter of time before Hainton Street is removed and Friargate and Littlefield Crossings are closed. The future also looks bleak for several of the others but as rumours of closure concerning almost all of these boxes have been heard from time to time it would not be appropriate to discuss which ones they might be.

Railway preservation came to the area in 1980 when the Grimsby-Louth Railway Preservation Society was formed with the aim of reopening the rail link between the two towns. Negotiations between the society and BR have been ongoing ever since but due to a road improvement scheme at the northern end of the line the present intention is to reopen the section from New Waltham southwards to Louth. Ever conscious of the massive investment this will require, initial plans are to open a steam centre at Ludborough – approximately half way – and then open the line in stages southwards before concentrating on the northern half of the line. One of the more ambitious projects the society has in hand is the removal of the station buildings at Bardney and transporting them to Louth for reconstruction adjacent to Louth North signal box. One can only wish them every success with their long, arduous and expensive task.

This chapter is partly one of gloom and despair and run down and closure as the rail network around Grimsby contracted. It has, however, survived. The aim of this book is to look nostalgically at the days of steam worked excursions and fish trains, the clanging of buffers and clanking and hissing of engines and because of this, details have been kept brief.

41 & 42. (Top and centre right) Great Coates Sidings, n.d. Exterior and interior views of Great Coates Sidings No. 2 signal box. This was one of the more remote signal boxes in Grimsby, being situated on the curve of the Grimsby District Light Railway at Pyewipe, just opposite Peter Dixons paper mill. It closed when goods traffic began to decline in the late 1960's and early 1970's. In the internal view signalman Les Bennett is seen sending a message on his telegraph instrument.

*Photo: GCRS and
R. Dane respectively*

43. (Below) Immingham, c.1966 This interesting aerial view shows the period of transition from steam to diesel at Immingham shed. The new diesel depot is nearing completion in the bottom centre of the view whilst, to the left, the remaining half of the steam shed is being converted into a wagon repair shop. The coaling tower is to the left of the steam shed and the coaling stage is at the back of the depot. To the right of the diesel depot is the dormitory block mentioned previously. Throughout this major rebuilding, Immingham remained in daily use as a diesel servicing depot. Dominating the dock area is the huge granary and both Eastern and Western Jetties can be seen protruding into the Humber.

Photo: Grimsby Evening Telegraph

44. Grimsby, East Marsh, c.1966. East Marsh goods yard as seen from New-market Street bridge. The Clee-thorpes line can be seen curving to the right into Grimsby Docks station with the Dock Offices immediately above the platforms and the Dock Tower to the right. The remains of Grimsby loco are on the extreme right with piles of coal already denoting its new use. Alongside the depot are container wagons for frozen food whilst on the opposite side of the main line, East Marsh yards are reasonably full and would appear to be employing three locomotives on pilot work. The goods shed on the left is part of Central Market Goods Depot, now closed.

There is an interesting story with regard to the building next to it alongside the diesel shunter. During an air raid in World War II, a bomb dropped alongside and, so the story goes, although little damage was incurred the building developed a list towards the crater, a defect which it retained until demolition. *Photo: R. Barnard*

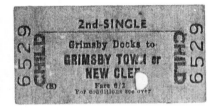

45. Grimsby, Pasture Street, c.1955. There is only one building that survives today from this view of Pasture Street level crossing and that is the coal office on the right. Class K2 2-6-0 No 61740 is rounding the curve from Garden Street with a semi-fast for Cleethorpes. The line running past the goods shed on the left is the link between the East Lincs line at Goods Junction and the docks.
Photo: J. McCulloch

46. Pasture Street, Grimsby, 1961. A period of change for the Pasture Street area. A new signalbox is under construction to replace both of the traditional structures, Pasture Street and Holme Street. These two boxes actually closed in early 1962 and with them went the familiar level crossing gates, Pasture Street's being replaced by barriers, and the sleepered crossing.
Photo B. Clark
courtesy Grimsby Public Libraries

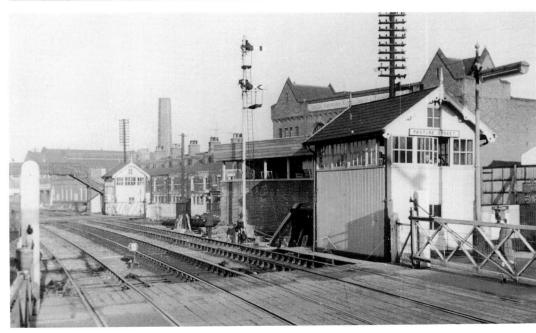

4 : The Clickety

The Immingham trams. Whenever the name is mentioned people who knew them tend to smile fondly as one does when thinking of a long lost friend. Gone are the memories of a journey on a cold winters night when the tram would shake, rattle, and roll its way alongside the frost or snow covered fields, its occupants thinking only of getting into the warmth of a mess room or putting their feet up beside a fire. Of being crammed like sardines for the six mile journey, at peak times, remaining upright simply because of the numbers of people in the car, or how hard the wooden swing back seats became after a few minutes. Time has softened the memory and all but a few express sadness at their passing.

The Grimsby District Electric Railway, as the GCR called it, was actually a part of the Grimsby District Light Railway, its building and route being part of the Light Railway Order passed in 1906.

The GCR awarded a contract to Price, Wills and Reeve for £11,360 to build a tramway across the open country between Pyewipe and Immingham in October 1909. The line was to run along the landward side of the light railway completed in 1906. At the same time and at a cost of £16,474, R. W. Blackwell & Co. were contracted to build the street tramway which would connect Pyewipe with Corporation Bridge, and to supply and fix the overhead wiring and bond the rails of the Pyewipe – Immingham section.

The original plans envisaged a triangular junction with the Great Grimsby Street Tramways at the junction of Freeport Wharf and Victoria Street. This junction would have given access to the centre of Grimsby and to Cleethorpes. However before this junction could be built it was essential that Corporation Bridge was replaced as it was not strong enough to support a tramway. The original structure had been built in 1869 and was designed by Charles Reboul Sacré, locomotive engineer of the MS&LR. The bridge was eventually replaced in 1928 by the one which survives today. By 1928 however, the tramway network in Grimsby was in decline and, therefore, the junction was never built. If it had, not only would there have been the prospect of GCR trams along the seafront at Cleethorpes and in the Old Market Place, Grimsby, but possibly a new generation of Grimsby Corporation single deck trams, the borough having taken over the GGST in 1926, might have been seen working to Immingham. A fascinating prospect and one that

may have prolonged the life of the borough tramways beyond the closing date of 1937. However, it was not to be and the terminus was built, and remained, on the Corporation Road side of Corporation Bridge.

The terminus was provided with a parcels office-cum waiting room, a building still existing and in use as a yacht chandlers attached to the nearby marina. Single track for the major part of its length, the terminus was double track although the line became single before it crossed Alexandra Road. From Corporation Bridge to Pyewipe the line ran as an ordinary street tramway with the rails set into the roadway along the centre of Corporation Road and Gilbey Road. From Pyewipe to Immingham the line resembled an ordinary railway line with the tracks being fixed to sleepers. Passing places were provided at Yarborough Street and Beeson Street along Corporation Road, and at Little Coates school and on the north side of Cleveland Bridge along Gilbey Road. From this point the line crossed into open country in a long left hand curve until it met the light railway.

The passing places on the country section were referred to by numbers and it was on this curve that No. 1 passing place was laid. The maintenance depot was constructed in the vee formed by the tramway and the light railway, and consisted of a two road, brick built, repair shop with a single track paint shop alongside. Three cars was the maximum that could be kept under cover at any one time and therefore the vehicles spent virtually their whole lives out in the open. Adjacent to the depot were three sidings and an inspection pit, the depot still surviving but in private ownership. Although never physically connected the tramway and the light railway ran side by side until they arrived at Queens Road, Immingham, where the tramway swung to the left to terminate alongside the road. The passing places along this section were as follows:— No. 2 was adjacent to the junction with the entrance to the maintenance depot, No. 3 at the point where Woad Lane, Great Coates crossed the tramway, Nos. 4 and 5 were opposite the present day Courtaulds works, No. 6 where Old Fleet Drain was crossed, No. 7 at Marsh Road crossing, Stallingborough, and No. 8 at the crossing of Kiln Lane, Stallingborough, the skeleton of a shelter surviving at this point. Nos. 3, 4, 6 and 7 passing places were removed as early as 1917.

47. Corporation Bridge, 28th August 1955. Ex Gateshead car 33 waits for its passengers to embark at Corporation Bridge terminus. The waiting room and parcels office have survived but in much changed form, and after various different uses are now home to a yacht chandlers.
Photo: the late J. E. Gready

48. Yarborough Street, n.d. Ex Gateshead car 31 is seen coming off the loop at Yarborough Street with a service to Immingham. Corporation Bridge is in the extreme distance. The wife of one of the authors lived in a house to the left of the tram and has fond memories of travelling on them during her first year at Little Coates school. The saddest part to this photograph is that not only has the tramway gone but the whole of the West Marsh was swept away in the early 1970's and a very individual and friendly community dispersed across the housing estates of Grimsby.

Photo: the late R. F. Mack

Aa **92334**
BRITISH TRANSPORT
COMMISSION (E)
Grimsby & Immingham
Electric Railway
Retain ticket for inspection

Mon		
Tues	RETURN	2
Wed	2/1	
Thur	SPECIAL	
Fri	CHEAP	1
Sat	DAY.	

For Conditions see over

49. Beeson Street, 10th June 1956. Entering the loop at Beeson Street, with the Duke of York Gardens (the Boulevard to locals) on the left is ex GCR car 4. The main reason for showing this view however, is on the left, the fascinating road sign. Signs such as this disappeared with the trams and informed other road uses of the approach of a loop and the fact that a tram in front of them was likely, literally, to pinch the road.

Photo: the late J. E. Gready

The length of the line from Corporation Bridge to Queens Road was 5⅜ miles and was opened on 15th May 1912. The original intention had been to run along the street section only and to provide a feeder to the steam railway service that was operating from Pyewipe. However, in 1909, as the steam service was just beginning to serve the public, the decision was taken to run the trams through to Immingham.

Power for the cars came from overhead wires and was generated by the power house on Immingham Dock and transmitted to the line through three substations. These were Immingham No. 3, near the grain silo on the docks, Pyewipe and the appropriately named Traction Substation. The third and latter was near to No. 6 passing place and the only one built solely for supplying current to the tramway, the other two also supplying power to dock installations.

In 1910 two extensions were authorised. One was a continuation of the tramway along Queens Road towards Immingham village, terminating adjacent to the entrance to the locomotive depot. Opened on 20th July 1915 it was, apparently, only used regularly for the first week after which a quarterly franchise car was the only traffic it saw. The overhead wiring on this section was dismantled in 1946 and the track lifted in 1955. One can only wonder why the GCR did not continue the line the short distance into Immingham itself as the potential traffic was certainly there and the population and local councils continuously requested this extension. Definitely a case of opportunity missed.

The second extension involved the reversal of the trams at Queens Road, at which point the line again became a street tramway and was double track. It crossed the light railway by means of a bridge and ran to the boundary of the dock estate where it crossed over to reserved land and followed the road along the river bank, terminating alongside the lock gates. This section, possibly the most important, opened without ceremony on 17th November 1913, a brick shelter surviving at the reversal point which was known as Immingham Town.

From the 30th June 1956 Grimsby Corporation exercised rights, provided for in the Light Railway Order of 1906, to purchase the section of line within its boundaries, and operations ceased between Corporation Bridge and Cleveland Bridge and so it was now only a matter of time before the remainder closed. However, the fight to keep it open was fought valiantly and managed to delay the fateful day for five years. The end came on Saturday 1st July 1961 when dozens of people turned out to say farewell to the Immingham trams.

The initial service left Corporation Bridge at 5.10 am and was followed at five minute intervals, by three more cars. The service then became hourly until 7.15 pm. There were fixed stops at Yarborough Street, Stortford Street and Little Coates school with conditional stops at Jackson Street, Beeson Street and No. 3 Passing Place (Great Coates). One can only assume that further stops were made on the country section on request. From Immingham the first car left at 5.45 am and an

50. Little Coates, 10th June 1956. Ex GCR car 4 has just descended Cleveland Bridge and is swaying into the loop at Little Coates school. Until their demise a few weeks later the trams were a part of everyday life along Gilbey and Corporation Roads. The sound of one rattling past could well have been one of the first sounds one of the authors heard as he was born in the front room of the house whose back garden is visible to the left of the tram.   *Photo: J. E. Gready*

hourly service was maintained until 7.45 pm. Between 5.30 pm and 6.30 pm the three additional cars which had travelled out from Grimsby in the morning returned. The journey took twenty minutes with a maximum speed of 12 mph being allowed along the street section and 25 mph on the country section. The fare was 5d(2½p). When the extension on to the docks opened, the journey time remained the same with the first car leaving Grimsby 5 minutes later at 5.15 am.

A 24 hour service soon came into operation although it was abandoned during the First World War. This service resuming upon the cessation of hostilities. A timetable for 1929 gives a good example of the services being offered in the inter war years. The first car of the day left Grimsby at 1.50 am, others following at 3 am, 4.15 am and 5.20 am. From then until 7.50 pm there was a half hourly service with two additional departures at 7.10 am and 8.30 am. After the 7.50 pm departure there was a break of one hour and then cars left at 8.50 pm, 9.20 pm, 9.50 pm, 10.30 pm, 10.50 pm (Saturdays excepted) and 11.30 pm. The service was much reduced on a Sunday, there being approximately 90 minutes between departures starting at 3 am. In the reverse direction the first car left at 12.20 am followed by others at 2.20 am, 3.45 am, 4.45 am and 5.50 am when the half hourly service commenced. The evening service after 8.20 pm was 9.20 pm, 10 pm, 10.20 pm, 11 pm and 11.20 pm (Saturdays excepted). Additional cars ran at 5 pm and 5.05 pm (Saturdays excepted) and there was a Saturdays only departure at

mid-day. The sunday service was similar to that from Grimsby but started at 12.20 am.

Between 10th September 1928 and 14th December 1929 there was also a 15 minutes service between Corporation Bridge and Stortford Street but this was replaced by a Grimsby Corporation bus service. The cheap day return fare in 1935 was one shilling (5p) whilst a workmens return was 7½d(3p).

Very few major alterations appear to have been made to the service over the years. A timetable for 1952 shows additional trams at 12.50 am from Grimsby and 1.20 am from Immingham. From 1956, when the street section closed, the first tram left Cleveland Bridge at 1 am and was followed by others at 2 am, 3.10 am, 4.25 am, 5.30 am, 6 am, 6.20 am, 6.30 am, 7 am, 7.20 am, 7.30 am, 8 am, 8.32 am, 8.38 am, 9 am and then half hourly until 11.30 pm. There was no departure at 8.30 pm. The Sunday service also started at 1 am with further cars at 2 am, 3.10 am, 4.45 am (Immingham Town only), 5.30 am, 7 am, 7.10 am, 7.30 am, 8.50 am, 9.30 am and then hourly until 11.30 pm. Additional cars ran at 4.50 pm, 5 pm and 6 pm. From Immingham the first weekday departure was 12.20 am followed by 1.22 am, 2.35 am, 4 am, 5.5 am, 5.55 am, 6.5 am, 6.35 am, 7.03 am, 7.24 am, 8.03 am, 8.15 am, 8.41 am, 9.03 am and then half hourly until midnight. Additional cars ran at 4.15 pm, 4.53 pm and 5.07 pm (both Saturdays excepted) and 5.21 pm. There were also

continued on page 43

51. Grimsby, 10th June 1956. Taken during the last month of operation of the Grimsby street section, ex Gateshead tram 31 is seen just after climbing Cleveland Bridge on a journey to Immingham. The vehicle appears to have stopped with its trailing bogie still on the incline and looks to be working an enthusiasts special. Cleveland Bridge is better known to locals as the "Tip", a name derived from its construction and which enabled Gilbey Road, along which the tramway ran, to cross the Great Coates branch without the need for a busy level crossing.   *Photo: J. E. Gready*

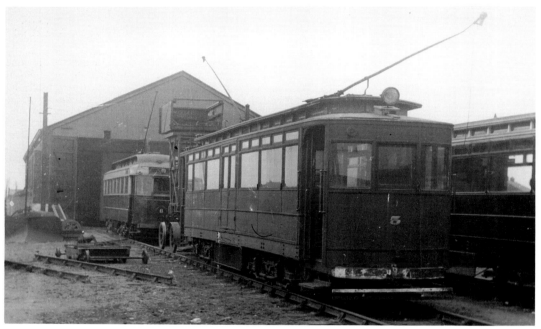

52. Cleveland Bridge, 29th May 1957.
Two Grimsby Corporation buses, an AEC Regent III RT type double decker and one of the pioneer dual entrance/exit AEC Reliances, both in the fondly remembered maroon and cream livery, wait for passengers at Cleveland Bridge terminus whilst ex GCR car 4 prepares to depart for Immingham. Cleveland Bridge became the Grimsby terminus a year earlier when the street service to Corporation Bridge ceased. The multitude of bicycles, with barely a lock between them, belong to some of the hundreds of workers who daily travelled from Grimsby to their jobs in Immingham. *Photo: J. H. Price*

53. Pyewipe, 15th August 1948. Four short cars, 40 instead of 64 seaters, were built for the connecting services with the Great Grimsby Street Tramways. As this service did not materialise these vehicles had a relatively short career and were withdrawn circa 1930, probably after the short lived service along Corporation Road and Gilbey Road ceased. They were all broken up with the exception of No. 5 which became a departmental vehicle and survived into the 1950's. It is seen here at Pyewipe depot along with one of the recently arrived Newcastle vehicles, No. 6. Although renumbered this vehicle still sports its old livery. Between the two trams is the overhead maintenance trolley which No. 5 and its successor, an ex Gateshead vehicle which carried the number DE320224, faithfully towed around the system. *Photo: J. H. Meredith*

54. Kiln Lane, Stallingborough, 29th September 1959. The rural peace of No. 8 Passing Place is briefly disturbed as ex Gateshead car 24 rattles through on a service to Grimsby. No. 8 Passing Place was at Kiln Lane, Stallingborough which was then a quiet country lane but is now part of a large industrial estate. *Photo: J. H. Price*

4: continued from page 41

additional cars on a Saturday lunchtime at 11.37 and 12.08. The Sunday service commenced at 12.35 am with further departures at 1.22 am, 2.45 am, 4.20 am, 5.10 am (from Immingham Town), 6.35 am, 8 am, 8.25 am, 10.05 am then hourly until midnight. Additional cars ran at 3.50 pm, 4.33 pm, 4.52 pm and 10.33 pm. However many departures required duplicate cars and a total of 19 vehicles were needed to sustain the service.

The timetable for 1957 shows additional departures from Cleveland Bridge at 6.50 am and 7.15 am on weekdays and 7.15 am on Sundays. From Immingham the weekday 7.03 am and 7.24 am departures disappeared to be replaced by a car leaving at 7.33 am. There was also an additional Sunday departure at 5.23 pm. This service continued in operation until 28th September 1959 when all services were withdrawn except at peak times and this was to continue until the line closed.

On the final day the normal peak times service operated during the morning. At 1.30 pm six cars left Cleveland Bridge in convoy with car No. 4 leading. This car carried a headboard bearing the legend "Grimsby – Immingham Electric Railway – Last Day July 1st 1961." The return departure time was booked as 2.03 pm which was kept precisely. The convoy left to the accompaniment of a fusilade of exploding detonators. Around 2.30 pm the last of the convoy arrived back at Cleveland Bridge and the tramway closed. An acquaintance has vivid memories of that last day and travelling with a friend they left Cleveland Bridge by one of the morning departures. Alighting at Immingham Town they paid a surreptitious visit to Immingham Loco before walking around the eastern side of the docks to the tram terminus. Arriving in the nick of time they boarded the first tram to leave, gaining the impression that the shed foreman was after them with a gun as the tram ran over the detonators. Being only 12 years old, the pair had never experienced the sound before. The fare on the last day was 2s 1d return.

In the 49 years that they ran the trams carried millions of passengers both to and from work and in 1957, when the end was in sight, they carried almost 800,000 people. One driver, reminiscing on the last day, recalled one night during the war when he counted 151 people aboard his tram. His car was one of six covering the last journey of the night and between them 1200 people were carried, the story going that some even sat on the fenders. During the severe winter of 1947 the trams were the only vehicles to get through to Immingham for several days, even the light railway alongside being impassable. One effect of the closure of the street section was the transfer of the huge number of bicycles, used by Grimsby people to get to their terminus, from Corporation Bridge to Cleveland bridge. In a morning they would be left in jumbled ranks as their owners hurried to get to work. At teatime the masses would return and how they found their own machine amidst all the others is anyone's guess, but find them they did. It would then be almost like a stampede as the hundreds of workers charged up Cleveland Bridge and down again to race pell mell down Gilbey Road. It was true to the saying, once seen never forgotten. The last tram along Corporation Road and Gilbey Road ran at 11.50 pm on 30th June 1956, though there were in fact two trams. The first was the normal departure and the second, car 4, carried local dignitaries and tram enthusiasts. Along both roads people stood on the pavement or in their gardens and waved them farewell. To most of these people it was the middle of the night but it was never too late to say goodbye to a friend.

To operate the service the GCR placed an order with Brush Electrical Engineering for four 54ft 2in long bogie cars (Nos. 1-4) and four 38ft 10in long bogie cars (Nos. 5-8). The long cars were capable of seating 72 in two compartments, one smoking and one non-smoking, containing 32 seats with 8 tip up seats in the central luggage compartment, and this was, apparently where the gambling fraternity passed the journey playing cards. The short cars had 48 seats in two compartments of 20, plus 8 additional seats in the central luggage compartment. The seats were made of wood strips and were of the swing back type. The cars presented a modern appearance at the time and the driver, whose driving position was also used for boarding the vehicles, had the luxury of an enclosed driving compartment with doors, something necessary for the country section but surprisingly uncommon on other tramways until the 1920's. Cars 1-8 were originally built without doors but these were fitted soon after entering service. Electrical equipment was supplied by Dick, Kerr and Co. In 1913 further long cars were needed and the GCR returned to Brush and Dick, Kerr for four identical vehicles (Nos. 9-12). The final purchase of cars made by the GCR in 1915 was again four long cars (Nos. 13-16) and although ordered from Brush they were built in the company's own works at Dukinfield. Equipment was again by Dick, Kerr.

It would appear that the original intention was to use the long cars on the Immingham service and the short cars on the link with the GGST. As the link was never built the short cars tended to be used only rarely at off peak times although it is believed that these were the vehicles which operated the short lived service to Stortford Street. After this service ceased there was little work for them and Nos. 6, 7 and 8 were withdrawn and scrapped in 1930. No. 5, however, was luckier and was converted into a repair vehicle in which form it lasted in service until 1952. The 12 long cars maintained the service until 1948 when, due to the expansion of industry along the Humber Bank it became necessary to obtain more vehicles. Had they survived the short cars would now have been invaluable.

Three cars were purchased from Newcastle upon Tyne Corporation

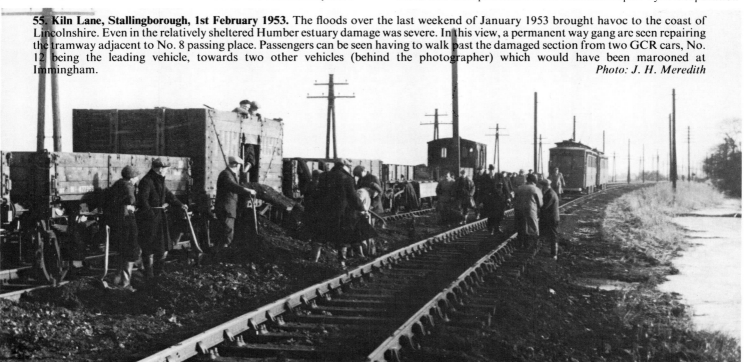

55. Kiln Lane, Stallingborough, 1st February 1953. The floods over the last weekend of January 1953 brought havoc to the coast of Lincolnshire. Even in the relatively sheltered Humber estuary damage was severe. In this view, a permanent way gang are seen repairing the tramway adjacent to No. 8 passing place. Passengers can be seen having to walk past the damaged section from two GCR cars, No. 12 being the leading vehicle, towards two other vehicles (behind the photographer) which would have been marooned at Immingham. *Photo: J. H. Meredith*

and took the numbers 6, 7 and 8. They looked antiquated and so they were. Built originally in 1901 by Hurst, Nelson they had been extensively rebuilt in 1932/33 by Newcastle Corporation. Electrical equipment was by Crompton, Parkinson and British Thomson Houston. The cars seated 40 in one compartment and were unique in that they were the only vehicles with upholstered seats to work on the tramway. They gave four years service before being withdrawn in 1952 and were broken up in 1955.

Faced with increasing passenger figures and an ageing fleet of cars the decision was taken in 1951 to purchase further vehicles. The new trams came from Gateshead and District Tramways Co., a total of 19 being apparently purchased but only 18 used. The numbers 17-33 and DE320224 were taken, this latter replacing car 5 as the repair car. They were known to tramway staff as Doodlebugs. Nos. 17, 21, 23, 28, 29, 32 and 33 were built by Brush and the remainder by the Gateshead Company in their own works between 1921 and 1928 and had seating for 48 with electrical equipment by Dick, Kerr.

As well as the ex Newcastle cars and car 5 four of the long cars were withdrawn on the arrival of the ex Gateshead vehicles. These were Nos. 2, 9, 10 and 13. On the night of 12th December 1948 two cars collided in thick fog 3 miles out of Grimsby. Visibility was down to 10 yards and 19 people were injured in the accident. A spare car was sent out from Grimsby to ferry the injured to Yarborough Street close to Grimsby General Hospital. Car 15 was apparently damaged in this accident but was repaired and returned to service, the identity of the other vehicle remains unknown. Cars 2 and 10 were damaged in another collision in the early 1950's and being beyond repair spent the remainder of their lives as store sheds at Pyewipe.

The remaining cars continued in service virtually until closure although car 11 had a lucky escape after colliding with an empty petrol tanker on Immingham Dock on the night of 17th November 1954. The driver and 4 passengers were injured by flying glass though none were detained in hospital and although the front of No. 11 was extensively damaged it was repaired. Shortly before closure however, No. 11 was again in the wars when it struck car 16 a glancing blow at No. 1 passing place, resulting in the withdrawal of both vehicles.

The 1959 reduction of services to peak times only resulted in the majority of the Gateshead cars being laid up for long periods. However No. 26 was surprisingly overhauled in 1960 and used occasionally afterwards. It was intended to use car 21 on the last day, but on the day before, after being carefully prepared, it was inadvertently backed into the depot doors, its place being taken by car 18 which was hurriedly swept out and spruced up.

After closure the cars were towed to Cleveland Bridge where they were stripped of everything of value and the remains unceremoniously burned. A sad end to loyal servants of fifty years standing. There is no doubt that the cars were worn out with many of them, including all the original GCR cars, having developed a sagging appearance at either end. However, as the Phoenix rises from the ashes, so did some of the cars survive the holocaust of their sisters. Car 20 is at Crich Tramway Museum and restored in its Gateshead livery as No. 5, Gateshead and District No. 10 at the Beamish Industrial Museum is the vehicle that received an overhaul in 1960, No. 26. What of the GCR cars? All but one perished at Cleveland bridge. No. 14 survives but sadly has been locked away in a shed at Clay Cross for many years, being too large to operate at Crich. It has been offered to Beamish, the Science Museum and NRM at York, all of whom have shown little interest and so it remains locked away. Surely, in these days of almost paranoid interest in local heritage, a place can be found for it where it belongs?

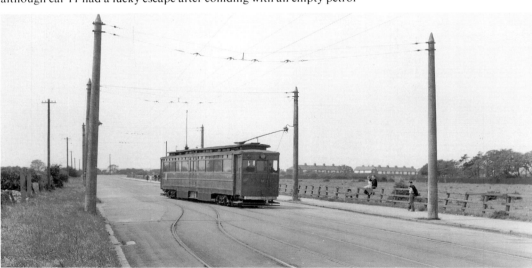

56. Immingham Town, 22nd July 1956
An interesting view of ex GCR car 14 negotiating the crossover at Immingham Town. The tram had just arrived from Grimsby via the line on the left and having reversed, changing tram poles in the process, is seen manoeuvring onto the right hand track to continue its journey to Immingham Dock. *Photo: T. J. Edgington*

57. Immingham Dock, 29th May 1957
The services to Immingham in a morning were intense and similarly the early evening return services. To save on wasted mileage the cars used on the morning service would be stored at Immingham during the day instead of returning to the depot at Pyewipe. It is these vehicles that are pictured here with four ex Gateshead cars, Nos. 27, 25, 22 and 31, in the foreground and an ex GCR car leading another line in the background. The GCR vehicle on the left hand track is on a scheduled service to Grimsby. In the right background is the coal hoist on the western jetty which by this date was approaching the end of its career.
Photo: J. H. Price

58. Immingham Dock, n.d. The terminus of the tramway at Immingham was adjacent to the lock gates, to the rear of the photographer. The waiting room is on the right of this view of two ex Gateshead vehicles, nos. 23 and 33. Judging by the number of people and their dress it is likely that the latter car has worked an enthusiasts special from Grimsby.
Photo: the late J. E. Gready

59. Grimsby & Immingham. The interior of GCR car No. 1 showing the wooden swing back seats and the driving position. When these vehicles were being broken up many of these seats were sold locally for as little as half a crown (12½p) and used as garden furniture. *Photo: B. Clark courtesy Grimsby Public Libraries*

60. Corporation Bridge, 21st June 1953. Four ex GCR long cars, 64 seaters, are lined up at Corporation Bridge on 21st June 1953. They are, left to right, Nos. 1, 11, 14 and 4. The replacement bridge, opened in 1928 and which would have carried the tramway over the Alexandra Dock, is in the background. Passing beneath car 1 is the railway line connecting the wood yards with Great Coates sidings. Railwaymen referred to the sidings to the right of the tram as New Ground whilst those to the left were Down the Farm. *Photo: J. H. Meredith*

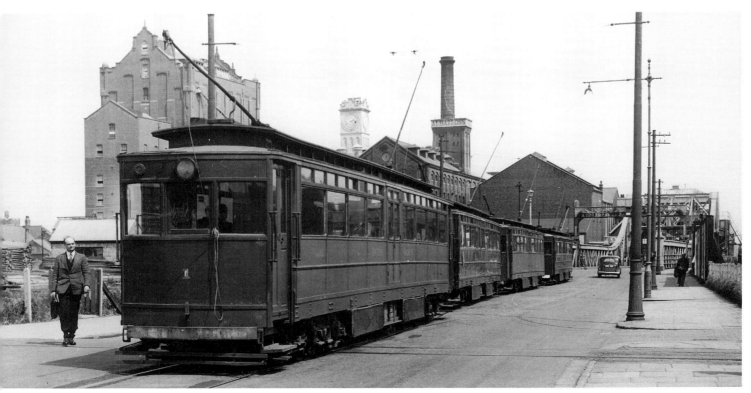

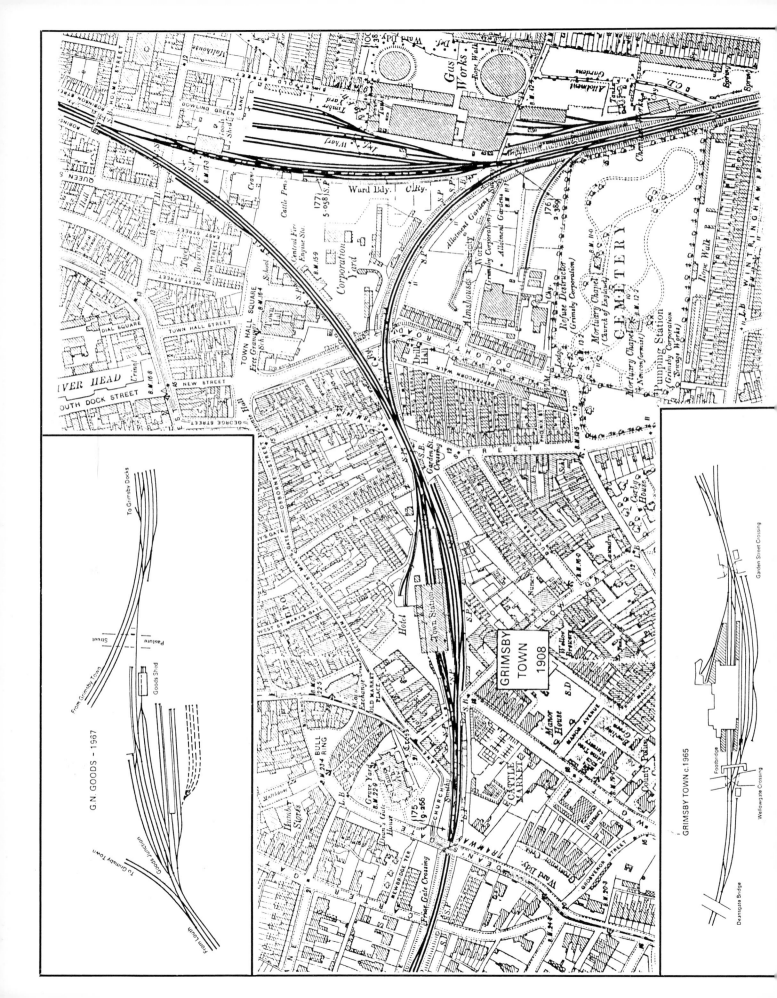

GRIMSBY TOWN 1908

G.N. GOODS - 1967

GRIMSBY TOWN c.1965

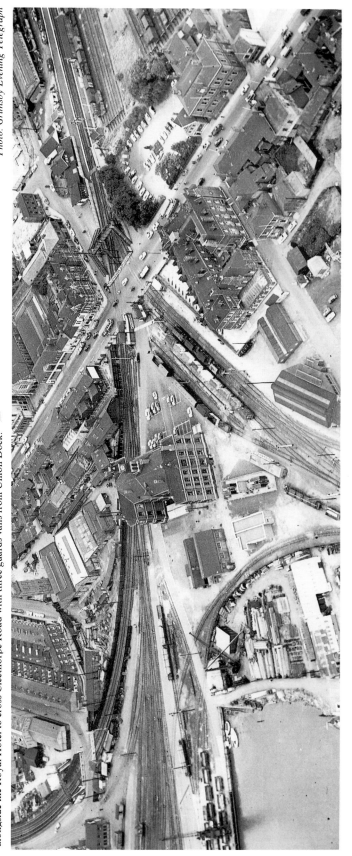

61. (Above) Grimsby, c.1960. The triangle of lines formed by Garden Street, Holme Street, and Goods Junctions is shown to good effect in this 1960 photograph. GN Goods appears to be busy with rows of box vans along the platforms and coal wagons in the sidings. Coal wagons can also be seen in the gas and electric works sidings alongside the East Lincs line, which runs in a straight line from Goods Junction towards the top right corner of the view. The sharp curve from Goods Junction to Garden Street is apparent and helps confirm that this section was an afterthought and the original station in Grimsby was planned for the East Marsh which is out of view to the left.
Photo: Grimsby Evening Telegraph

62. (Below) Grimsby, c.1961. The central features of this 1961 photograph are the Dock Offices and, to the right of it, the Royal Hotel. Grimsby Docks station is in the top right corner with East Marsh sidings to the right of it and the Railway Hotel to the left. Opposite the Royal Hotel, in the car park, is the statue of Prince Albert which now stands in front of the Dock Offices. The line to Cleethorpes curves away in the top left corner across Fish Dock Road level crossing. Riby Street Platforms would have been under the footbridge at this point. A diesel shunter is visible waiting alongside the Royal Hotel to cross Cleethorpe Road with three guards vans from Union Dock.
Photo: Grimsby Evening Telegraph

5 : The Grand Tour

63. Grimsby, c.1952. There is a saying that every picture tells a story. This one relates a history. The whole reason for the growth of Grimsby is encapsulated in this one view. The Royal Dock and the Union Dock are on the left and the Fish Docks are on the right.

The coaling jetty built into the Royal Dock is being fed by conveyor from wagons that are being tipped alongside the Union Dock almost level with Union Dock signal box. The large transit shed on the west side of the dock is surrounded by railway lines whilst above it, level with the Dock Tower, is the Pier station building which became an emigrants home soon after being built. Towards the centre of the view are the Dock Offices and the Royal Hotel with Cleethorpe Road running past the hotel from bottom left to centre right. Grimsby Docks station is adjacent to Cleethorpe Road level crossing with the Railway Hotel to its right. To the left of the station is East Marsh goods yard and below the station buildings are the wagon repair shops, now Fowler and Holden Ltd. Immediately below this building is Grimsby loco shed with three of its tracks still under cover but looking in a fairly run down state of repair. Also note in the bottom right hand corner the circle where the turntable was once situated.

Returning to the Royal Dock, the yards along its east side can be seen fanning outwards, those on the left serving the Royal Dock whilst those to the right were used for assembling fish trains. Numerous sidings led from these yards to various parts of the Pontoon, the covered area which runs along the whole western side of the Fish Docks from a point level with the Dock Tower to a point vertically in line with the loco shed. Keen observers will also note that one of the Humber ferries is in the dry dock adjacent to the Dock Tower and that there are several more sidings containing fish vans to

the right of this dock. Immediately above the dry dock, in the Royal Dock basin, is the herring quay which would see hectic use for the few short weeks of the year that the herring shoals were passing the mouth of the Humber on their annual migration around Britains coastline.

Fish vans are visible, being loaded at the point where the Pontoon takes a 90 degree turn to the right. Continuing along this stretch of the Pontoon it is also possible to see loaded fish vans on their way to New Clee for marshalling into trains while more empty vans are waiting their turn to be moved alongside the quay. To the right of these, Humber Bridge Road is visible crossing the railway and above the bridge the coal sidings and coal hoists for the bunkering of the trawlers can just be identified.

Through all of this runs the railway to Cleethorpes. Entering the picture in the bottom right hand corner adjacent to the loco shed it is already between the platforms of Docks station and runs in a straight line towards the Dock Offices. Here it begins a sharp turn to the right to cross Fish Dock Road and pass between the closed Riby Street platforms, which are just visible. The line continues this curve until, adjacent to the bottom left corner of the Pontoon, it begins a reverse curve which takes it parallel with the Fish Dock but separated from it by a row of fish houses. At the point where the line meets those coming from the Pontoon it again curves right to pass under Humber Bridge Road and into New Clee station, just out of view in the top right of the photograph.

What of a similar view today? The Royal Hotel has gone, swept away with the building of Cleethorpe Road flyover. There are still several sidings along the west side of the Royal Dock plus a few more, overgrown, at East Marsh. Otherwise, all that remains of the railway is the single track to Cleethorpes. This photograph was taken in the early 1950's but even fifteen years later little would have changed. However, the fifteen years that followed were the most destructive, in railway terms, that the area has ever known.   *Photo: E. Green*

64. Barton, 28th April 1954. Former GCR Class 9F, (later LNER Class N5), 0-6-2T 69305 is seen at the head of the branch train at Barton. To the left is a guards van which is on the line leading to a coal yard whilst on the right is the goods platform complete with canopy. Out of view to the right is the goods shed which was at right angles to the branch and was reached via a wagon turntable.

Photo: D. Lee Photography

65. Barton, c.1905. Passenger traffic on the Barton branch has never been heavy although most photographs show reasonably lengthy trains, the reason for this being that the stock would have worked a Cleethorpes – New Holland train and before returning would also work a trip down the branch. The same applied to the locomotives and it was not uncommon to see one of the GCR's former top link machines ekeing out its final few years on such turns. There being no turntable at Barton these engines would be required to work tender first in one direction, most unpleasant for the crews when the wind was blowing a gale off the nearby River Humber, especially if it was raining at the same time. From time to time the branch was subjected to attempts at reducing running costs. One such example is seen here with GCR steam railmotor No. 1 awaiting passengers for New Holland. In the early 1950's a GWR diesel railcar was tested on various unremunerative services in the area including this branch and the Louth – Grimsby motor trains.

Photo: D. Lee Photography

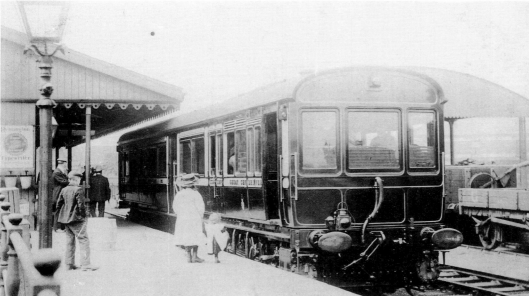

66. Barrow Haven, 24th September 1962. Barrow Haven halt was the only intermediate station on the Barton branch. The meagre facilities are seen here looking towards New Holland on 24th September 1962. At least intending passengers could shelter in the booking hall which backed onto the Humber whereas today they have to use the basic shelter perched on the platform which receives the full force of the wind and rain off the river.

Photo: D. Thompson

The Pier, New Holland

67. (Above) New Holland, c.1932. A strong wind appears to be blowing off the river judging by the direction of the smoke from the chimney of Class J21 0-6-0 No. 289. The engine is alongside the coaling stage at New Holland depot, the doors of which are visible behind the loco's tender. The carriages in the background are in the sidings alongside the Grimsby – New Holland line. The photograph can be dated to 1932 when this locomotive and a sister engine spent nine months at the depot during a rather nomadic spell that saw them allocated to several depots in the southern area of the LNER. They had originally been built for the North Eastern Railway.

Photo: N. E. Stead

68. New Holland, c.1898. Sacré Class 12A 2-4-0 No. 360 is seen crossing from the down to the up line on New Holland Pier in the closing years of the last century. The masts of a sailing ship can just be seen in the dock in the left background whilst visible along-side the locomotive is the funnel of one of the humber ferries. Note the mostly wooden structure of the upper part of the pier.

Photo: D. Lee Photography

69. New Holland Pier, 3rd June 1952. The Paddle Steamer *Lincoln Castle* waits for departure in the background whilst nearer the camera a permanent way man is busily engaged in his work. Meanwhile, a driver leans against the railings of the pier prior to boarding his engine, Class A5 4-6-2T No. 69820, which will depart with the 1.45 pm to Immingham. A timeless scene now gone forever.

Photo: T. J. Edgington

70. New Holland Town, 24th September 1962. New Holland Town station looking towards Grimsby on 24th September 1962. The retaining walls for the original overall roof can be seen on both platforms together with the canopy on the up and the shelter on the down platforms which replaced it. After closure of the ferry service the station was razed to the ground and a fertilizer plant now occupies the site. Rails still run along the pier and a small industrial shunter provides the motive power. *Photo: D. Thompson*

71. New Holland Town, c. 1946. In order to honour the memory of railway employees who gave their lives in the Great War, several railway companies endowed one of their locomotives with an appropriate name. In the case of the GCR, it was one of J. G. Robinson's new Class 9P 4-6-0's, No. 1165, which took the name *Valour*. The nameplate was also inscribed with a suitable memorial. During the 1920's this locomotive would haul a special train on armistice day to Sheffield where a service was performed at the GCR's war memorial at Victoria station. The locomotive, on these occasions, would also carry wreaths on its smokebox door and on its nameplates. *Valour* is seen here as LNER Class B3 No. 1498 entering New Holland Town with a stopping train from Cleethorpes in the twilight of its career. The Barton branch can be seen curving away to the right with the Grimsby – Barton line running across the background. Above the first coach is the Yarborough Arms Hotel. *Photo: D. Lee Photography*

72. New Holland. c.1960. A British Railways 204hp 0-6-0 diesel shunter is seen here outstationed at a derelict New Holland locoshed, the view being towards Barton. *Photo: N. E. Stead*

73. (Right) Goxhill station, c.1920.
This view of Goxhill shows the up, Grimsby, platform. The station building with its tall chimneys and stone pillared windows was typical of the stations built for the opening of the line. The junction for the Barton and Immingham Light Railway was a little distance beyond the signal box.
Photo: D. Lee Photography

74. (Above) Goxhill, August 1961. In this view, looking towards New Holland, the building on the down line platform can also be seen. This station, unlike the others north of Habrough, retains all of its buildings although those on the up platform are in private hands and those on the down platform are derelict. Until recently there were only three road overbridges between Cleethorpes and New Holland, at Humber Street and Deansgate in Grimsby and at Goxhill. The last mentioned can just be seen beyond the dmu.
Photo: G. Biddle

75. (Right) Thornton Abbey, n.d. A Victorian view of Thornton Abbey with a New Holland – Cleethorpes train entering the station. The locomotive is MS&L 0-4-2 269 built in 1864 and one of three engines loaned and then bought from the Mid-Wales Railway in July 1869 for an all in price of £5,000. There is an abundance of agricultural traffic in the sidings. The abbey after which the station was named is across open fields on the right and provides a superb view from the carriage window.
Photo: D. Lee Photography

76 & 77. Ulceby (dates in caption). Ulceby station, like so many others on Britain's railways, was named after the nearest village but not actually built there. Of standard New Holland line design, this station, which once boasted refreshment rooms and was the exchange point for Grimsby when the expresses ran to New Holland, has been swept away and replaced by a small wooden platform built on top of the old up platform, on the right. In the upper view a Brush Type 2 diesel is seen passing through the station on 21st April 1966 with a train of coal empties from Immingham. The train is signalled onto the left hand fork at the junction which would take the train to Brocklesby and the west. This line is the northern arm of the Ulceby – Brocklesby – Habrough triangle. The lines immediately in front of the camera are the eastern arm of the triangle and lead to Habrough. The junction for the Humber Commercial Railway is visible beyond the station in the lower view, taken on 28th September 1962, and it is from this line that the train in the upper view had come. Until the opening of the nearby A180 trunk road there was, for several years, a temporary road bridge crossing the line between the signalbox and the station to cater for the volume of road traffic using the route to and from Immingham. Since the opening of the A180 this bridge has been removed.

Photos: H. B. Priestley and D. Thompson respectively

78. (Below) Brocklesby, 28th September 1962. The junction of the lines from Ulceby, on the left, and Habrough, on the right, are visible in the middle distance of this view of Brocklesby station. It is interesting to note that the relief lines were not accessible from both directions at the junction, with trains on the down relief having to take the left hand fork for Ulceby whilst trains for the up relief line could only be travelling from Habrough. There were, however, connections between these lines west of Brocklesby station. *Photo: D. Thompson*

79. Brocklesby, c.1958. Class D11 4-4-0 No. 62670 *Marne* passing Brocklesby station with an excursion for Cleethorpes. Several members of the "Director" class were named after battles in the Great War, this loco being an example. It is also notable in being the last new locomotive built for the Great Central Railway, entering service a few days before the grouping in December 1922.

Photo: N. E. Stead

80. Brocklesby, August 1961. The station frontage at Brocklesby in August 1961 showing the proximity of the up relief line to the buildings.

Photo: R. E. G. Read
courtesy G. Biddle

81. Brocklesby, September 1964. A Class O4 2-8-0 is seen taking the avoiding line past Brocklesby station with a mixed goods for Immingham. The train is on the down relief line which, together with the up relief line, on the extreme left, was opened in 1915. The up relief line is the one referred to in the text as passing the front door of the stationmasters house. In recent months these relief lines have been subject to systematic removal. *Photo: C. J. Paine*

82 & 83. (top and centre) **Brocklesby, 27th March 1907.** The area has fortunately been free from serious railway accidents over the years. There have been numerous bumps and scrapes but by far the most destructive incident occurred at Brocklesby on the 27th March 1907 when a coal train and a fish train collided within the station area, one of the locomotives, Class 15 2-6-0 No. 966 built by Baldwins in the USA, being so badly damaged it had to be scrapped. These two views show a part of the scene shortly afterwards. In the upper view fish and fish barrels can be seen piled on the platform whilst beyond is the remains of a locomotive tender. In the lower view one of the locomotives, probably No. 966, can be seen laid on its side beneath a pile of wreckage.
Photos: Welholme Galleries

84. Melton Ross, 6th August 1962. With the exception of the coastal belt from Cleethorpes through to Killingholme the railways covered by this book traverse a rural, heavily agricultural, area. At Melton Ross, however, agriculture and industry come together, the line passing between old and new limestone workings at this point. Ardsley based Class B1 4-6-0 No. 61110 is seen at Melton Ross on 6th August 1962 with an excursion from West Yorkshire, with some of the new limestone workings visible in the background. *Photo. J. Willerton*

85. (Above) Barnetby, n.d. The village of Barnetby can be seen in the distance as Class B1 4-6-0 No. 61405 sets out along the quadrupled section of track towards Brocklesby with an excursion for Cleethorpes. The line traces a natural gap in the Wolds at this point and is the reason why trains take a northward route out of Grimsby instead of heading directly westwards. Although circuitous this route was infinitely more economical than boring long tunnels or building steep gradients which a line leading directly westwards from Grimsby would have required. *Photo: N. E. Stead*

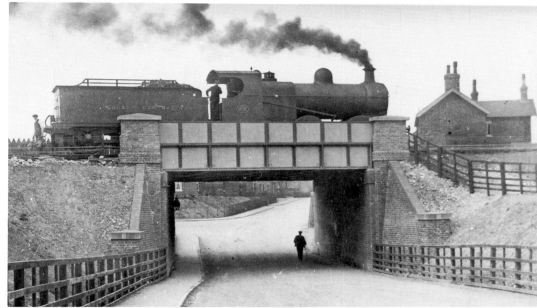

86. Barnetby, c.1914. GCR Class 9J 0-6-0 No. 976 poses on the new overbridge at Queens Road, Barnetby in 1914. These locos were nicknamed "Pom Poms" as the staccatto beat of their exhaust could be likened to the sound of the gun of the same name. They became LNER Class J11. Shortly after these locomotives were introduced, J. G. Robinson built a similar class with a 4-4-0 wheel arrangement for express passenger work. These speedy machines, because of their similarity to the 9J's, became known as the Pom Pom Bogies by railwaymen and enthusiasts alike. They became LNER Class D9 and an example can be seen on page 9. *Photo: GCRS Collection*

87. Barnetby, c.1910. The east end of the station at Barnetby before the widening of 1912. The original East signalbox is on the left and Queens Road crosses the railway on the level. After rebuilding, the signalbox was positioned out of view on the left and as can be seen above Queens Road became a subway. *Photo: GCRS Collection courtesy Welholme Galleries*

88. (Left) Barnetby, 5th August 1964. Class 8F 2-8-0 No. 48632 is heading an empty fish train through Barnetby in this view taken on 5th August 1964. Barnetby West signal box is clearly visible on the right of this view whilst evidence of track rationalisation is visible on the signal gantry where some of the signals have large crosses on them indicating that they are out of use. The 8F was not a stranger to the area as, although an LMS design, several were allocated to Immingham towards the end of World War II and for a couple of years afterwards. Seventy were actually purchased by the LNER but were exchanged in 1947 for Austerity type 2-8-0's returning from war duty. *Photo: J. Hewson*

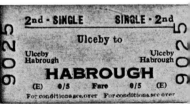

89. (Left) Barnetby, 5th August 1964. Did you know that "Spaceships" were once a common sight in this part of the world? Class 9F 2-10-0 No. 92095 is seen passing Barnetby station with a train of empty coal wagons for the Nottinghamshire coalfield. To those busily engaged in searching this photograph for a UFO perhaps we should explain that "spaceship" is one of the nicknames endowed upon the Class 9F locos. East signal box can be seen above the centre of the train whilst on the right is Barnetby's water tower which was built in 1849 by C. E. Williams & Co. of Leeds. This tower survived the rebuilding of 1912 and only fell into disuse when steam locomotives disappeared from the scene. It has since been demolished. *Photo: J. Hewson*

90. (Left) Habrough, 29th July 1962. The Habrough – Brocklesby and Habrough – Ulceby lines actually ran parallel for several hundred yards before forming a junction immediately north of Habrough station. Class B1 4-6-0 No. 61317 rounds the curve from Ulceby with a New Holland – Cleethorpes semi-fast. The line to Brocklesby can be seen on the left. *Photo: J. Willerton*

91. (Above) Habrough, n.d. Class K3 2-6-0 61846 at Habrough on a slow train to Cleethorpes. *Photo: N. E. Stead*

92. (Right) Habrough, c.1947. Class J11 0-6-0 No. 4421 clatters over the junction at Habrough with a New Holland – Cleethorpes semi-fast. The strange layout of this junction is clearly visible behind the train. Effectively, the up main line became the down main line and the down main line became the down New Holland line. This interesting layout came into being when Cleethorpes became the eastern terminus of the main line. Before then the New Holland line ran straight with the main line on a turn out. Recent rationalisation has caused the main line to now run straight on whilst the New Holland line, which has been singled between Habrough and Ulceby, is on a turn out. *Photo: L. Brown courtesy N. E. Stead*

93. (Right) Little London Level Crossing. Class D11 4-4-0 No. 62668 *Jutland* passing Little London level crossing with the empty stock for a New Holland – Cleethorpes train on 25th July 1959. This crossing was the first in the area to be replaced by automatic half barriers in the early 1960's, the gatehouse being demolished shortly afterwards. *Photo: J. Willerton*

94. (Above) Stallingborough, August 1961. Stallingborough station looking towards New Holland in August 1961. Another of the standard New Holland line stations as far as the main buildings are concerned although those on the down platform are similar to Habrough rather than Ulceby or Goxhill. *Photo: G. Biddle*

95. Healing, c. 1913. A truly sylvan scene of the approach to the station taken shortly before the first world war. This view seems to typify the truly rural atmosphere of so many branch and secondary main lines throughout Britain which were swept away with the rationalisation and closures of the 1960's. A scene that has virtually disappeared forever except perhaps at places such as Healing. Very little has changed in the intervening years.
Photo: Welholme Galleries

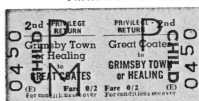

96. Healing, c.1905. An unidentified MS&LR 4-4-0 is approaching Healing station in the early years of the twentieth century. Judging by the number of people on the platform it would appear that something special was happening, perhaps an outing or a visit by someone of importance. Note the sidings alongside the down platform which are referred to in the text.
Photo: Courtesy Grimsby-Louth RPS

97 (Above) Great Coates, n.d. Young trainspotters peer through the level crossing gates as Class D11 4-4-0 No. 62666 *Zeebrugge* approaches Great Coates with an excursion. Photographs of excursion trains feature strongly in this book as, up to the mid 1960's, people from all over Yorkshire and the North Midlands visited Cleethorpes in their thousands and almost all came by train. On one August Bank Holiday Monday in the late 1950's there were over 40 excursions with a total of 99 over the three days of the holiday period.

Photo: Photographer unknown

98. Great Coates, 26th September 1963. Diesel multiple units came early to the New Holland line services although even into the 1960's it was still possible to find a B1 rostered to work the line. Such an occasion is captured here as Class B1 4-6-0 No. 61284 is seen running into Great Coates with a train from New Holland on 26th September 1963. Note that a porter is waiting to assist passengers wishing to alight, a courtesy that would soon disappear as all but the main stations became unstaffed halts.

Photo: B. J. Miller

99. Great Coates, 18th May 1964. Class B1 4-6-0 No. 61329 enters Great Coates station with a Cleethorpes – Doncaster stopping train on 18th May 1964. It is passing the site of the cattle dock. Within a few years the short run from Marsh Junction to Great Coates was to change dramatically with Grimsby's need for new housing and industrial land, the open land in the right background being developed into the large Willows housing estate. *Photo: C. J. Paine*

100. (Left) Killingholme, 24th September 1962. The only station on the Barton & Immingham not featured so far was at Killingholme and was another example of the station being named after the nearest village which was some distance away. The meagre facilities were more than sufficient for the traffic the line attracted and it was no surprise when the passenger service was withdrawn from the 17th June 1963. This part of the line still sees regular use however as oil storage tanks are sited along the trackside. *Photo: D. Thompson*

101. (Below) Immingham, c.1962. Immingham Dock station from the air almost disappears amidst the oil tanks and ship repair facilities. It is in the bottom right hand corner of this 1962 view with a DMU awaiting departure. The girder bridges, originally built to carry coal wagons out to the Western Jetty, are in the top right hand corner and have found a new lease of life carrying an oil pipeline. The railway can be seen snaking through the centre of the picture on its way to Immingham West Junction.
Photo: Grimsby Evening Telegraph

102. (Left) Immingham Dock, June 1969. Immingham Dock station is seen here in June 1969, four months prior to closure. Note that the platform is of concrete construction and that the basic facilities are of totally different materials and design. When it is considered that this station backs directly onto the River Humber it was a little surprising to find both buildings still standing and in reasonable condition during a visit in 1987. The platform is also complete but the trackbed is now a car park.
Photo: Grimsby Public Libraries

103. (Above) Immingham, c.1959. Immingham depot viewed from the coaling tower during the period that the roof was being replaced. On the left is the coaling stage with, above it, the water tank and the water softening plant at the rear. After the coaling tower was built the coal stage tended to be used for locos requiring better grade coal for the depots prestige jobs whilst the tower dispensed coal for all other duties. *Photo: J. McCulloch*

104. Immingham M.P.D., 3rd May 1964. There was less than two years left for steam locomotives at Immingham when this view of visiting Class O1 2-8-0 No. 63590 was taken. It is seen at the west end of the depot on 3rd May 1964. What is most noticeable, however, when compared with the other views of the depot, is the new, somewhat austere, roof.
Photo: C. J. Paine

105. Immingham M.P.D., c.1934. Great Central locomotives feature strongly throughout this book and by far the most graceful of these are J. G. Robinson's Atlantics, nicknamed Jersey Lilies. Altogether, 31 were built of which 4 appeared as compound rather than simple engines. These four took their place in the front line of express work alongside their simple propulsion sisters. They were based initially at Gorton (Manchester) and then Leicester. By May 1933, all four had progressed to Immingham where they operated services to Lincoln, Doncaster, Sheffield and New Holland, until withdrawn in 1947. One of this quartet, LNER Class C5 4-4-2 No. 5365 *Sir William Pollitt*, is seen at the east end of Immingham shed in the 1930's. *Photo: G. Willerton courtesy J. Willerton*

106, 107, 108. Immingham M.P.D.
These three views show the east end of
Immingham shed under three different owners. The top view was taken in
GCR days when the shed was newly
built, with a Class J11 0-6-0 and Class
O4 2-8-0 awaiting their next turn of
duty. Taken about thirty years later,
the centre view shows the depot
towards the end of its LNER ownership. Standing adjacent to the
sheerlegs is Class J11 0-6-0 4305
whilst a Class K3 2-6-0 and a Class
O4 are amongst the engines in front
of the shed. The lower view was taken
about ten years later, in BR days, and
shows how the state of the shed roof
had deteriorated. It was replaced
shortly afterwards. Class B1 4-6-0
No. 61408 is facing the camera with
B1, K3 and WD 8F's facing the depot.
*Photographs: Welholme Galleries,
R. H. G. Simpson, J. McCulloch*

ENGINE SHEDS IMMINGHAM

109. Immingham Dock, c.1923. Two of the coal hoists in operation on the South Quay in the 1920's. Both private and company owned wagons are visible on the quayside below the approach to the hoists. Note the extensive use of concrete.

Photo: Welholme Galleries

110. Immingham Dock, 12th July 1906. For the turning of the first sod ceremony on 12th July 1906, the contractors provided luxurious rolling stock in the shape of open wagons fitted with benches for the less important visitors to observe the goings on. This view was taken in what was to become the bed of the new dock shortly after the thunderstorm mentioned in the text, with the contractors 0-6-0ST *Morecambe* at the head of the train. Note the crude, but efficient way, of de-training.

Photo: Welholme Galleries

111. (Below) Stallingborough, 24th May 1961. 350hp 0-6-0 diesel shunter D3159 is heading for Immingham along the Grimsby District Railway at Kiln Lane, Stallingborough on 24th May 1961. Although many photographs were taken along the tramway, on the left of this view, very few were taken of locomotives working along the light railway adjacent to it.

Photo: J. H. Price

112. Great Coates Sidings, n.d. In this view, taken adjacent to Great Coates Sidings No. 2 box, the severe curvature of the light railway is readily apparent. The line enters the view under Cleveland Bridge, on the left, and curves through ninety degrees alongside the tram terminus, the small wooden building in the centre of the photograph, to pass along the right hand side of the wagons in the right foreground. The rear of Great Coates Sidings No. 1 signal box is visible alongside Cleveland Bridge whilst to its right, behind the diesel shunter in the distance, coaling facilities were provided in the form of a primitive wooden coaling stage with a water crane alongside. Note the number of men engaged in shunting, in particular the two who appear to be riding on the framing of the diesel shunter, just visible behind the timber wagons in the foreground.
Photo: R. Dane

113. Great Coates Sidings, c.1931. Class O4 2-8-0 No. 6621 appears to be banking a train around the curve between Great Coates No. 1 Sidings and Great Coates No. 2 Sidings signal boxes. In fact the loco has probably just arrived at West Marsh sidings with its train and has run round it in order to propel it into Great Coates sidings, which are out of view on the right. On the extreme left is the chimney of the Grimsby Fish Meal Co's. factory whilst in later years Peter Dixons used the fields on the right for the storage of wood pulp. Today a view from the same vantage point, Cleveland Bridge, would be barely recognisable as the A180 trunk road crosses the railway on a high bridge just beyond the signal post in the centre of the view. *Photo: N. Camplejohn*

114. (Left) West Marsh, April 1930. West Marsh sidings, between Cleveland Bridge and Marsh Junction, have survived the ravages of the 1960's and 1970's and still see limited use although the trackwork is much reduced. In this April 1930 view the sidings appear partially empty as a Class J11 0-6-0 passes by on the Great Coates branch with a van train for the docks and a Class J39 0-6-0 awaits its turn to follow with a coal train. *Photo: N. Camplejohn*

115. (Left) West Marsh, April 1931.
A mighty Class K3 2-6-0, No. 127, has been seconded to work a transfer freight in this April 1931 view of West Marsh sidings. The locomotive is heading tender first along the Great Coates branch towards Marsh Junction and is probably bound for one of the yards on the east side of Grimsby. West Marsh sidings have always been known locally as Congo, one assuming because the marshiness of the area can be likened to an African jungle. The fields in the background are now part of the South Humberside Industrial Estate and a cold store obliterates the view immediately beyond the railway. *Photo: N. Camplejohn*

116. (Above) Marsh Junction, 12th April 1962. A strong wind is blowing off the Humber as Class O2 2-8-0 63941 approaches Marsh Junction with Frodingham – High Dyke (Grantham) iron ore empties on 12th April 1962. The smoke from the loco is being blown across what is now the site of the Willows housing estate which like those on the right was open fields when this view was taken. The South Humberside Industrial Estate now covers the fields on the right. The western arm of the Marsh Junction triangle can be seen diverging to the right. *Photo: P. Loftis*

117. (Left) Grimsby-Littlefield Lane, 3rd March 1961. Class K3 2-6-0 No. 61944 is about to cross Littlefield Lane on 3rd March 1961 with an empty fish train from Banbury. This train would have been assembled overnight at Banbury and contained vans returning from the West Country, the south coast, and the South Midlands. The Banbury fish was normally a Woodford Halse turn but on this occasion it is being hauled by an Immingham locomotive. *Photo: J. Willerton*

118. Grimsby-Littlefield Lane, c.1936. Excursion trains ran to Cleethorpes almost from the time the line opened. This view, taken in 1936, typifies the pre-war scene. The rolling stock is already of a bygone age and consists of six wheel carriages dating from the last century. The engine too is no spring chicken with LNER Class B5 4-6-0 No. 6070 being built by the GCR in 1902, primarily for working the fast fish trains out of Grimsby.

Photo: E. R. Morten

119. Grimsby, 16th March 1961. Between Littlefield and Friargate Crossings the line began a long left hand curve which continued as far as Grimsby Town station. Although spring is just around the corner the trees along Queens Parade show little sign of new foliage in this 16th March 1961 view of Class 9F 2-10-0 92194 ambling tender first towards Grimsby Docks to pick up a fish train. WD Class 8F 2-8-0 90139 can be seen approaching with a High Dyke – Frodingham iron ore train.

Photo: J. Willerton

120. Grimsby, 3rd August 1958. The summer months brought about a tremendous change to this section of line. The trees along both Queens Parade and Princes Avenue being covered in lush greenery made it an almost idyllic spot to while away a Sunday morning observing the incoming excursions. With Littlefield Lane in the distance Class B1 4-6-0 61285 is approaching Friargate with an excursion on 3rd August 1958.

Photo: J. Willerton

121. (Above) Grimsby-Friargate, c.1955. A Sheffield – Cleethorpes train crossing Friargate behind Class B1 4-6-0 61231.
Photo: J. McCulloch

122. Grimsby-Friargate, September 1937. The 6.16 am Doncaster – Cleethorpes and the 10.50 am return working were normally trains that aroused little interest amongst the railway fraternity. However, on the mornings of 21st-23rd September 1937 people who normally paid little attention to railways flocked to the lineside to watch these trains pass, the reason being that they were hauled by a streamliner. Although the first of Gresleys A4's were little more than two years old their feats on the East Coast main line were already becoming legendary and to see such an engine on a secondary line such as that between Doncaster and Cleethorpes was unique. What the lineside observers saw on those mornings 50 years ago was not one of the famed A4's but the rebuilt Class B17 4-6-0's which had been streamlined to work the new East Anglian express between Liverpool Street and Norwich. The rebuilding was carried out at Doncaster from where locomotives were normally run in on turns to Grantham. For some reason, however, they were put onto a Cleethorpes turn and No. 2859 *East Anglian* is seen leaving Grimsby on the morning of Wednesday 22nd September 1937 with the 10.50 am to Manchester. The other loco No. 2870 *City of London*, worked the same turn the next day.
Photographer unknown

123. Grimsby Town, c.1958. This view, taken from Deansgate in the late 1950's, shows the western approach to Grimsby Town station. The station is just visible in the middle distance under Wellowgate footbridge as Class B1 4-6-0 61318 weaves its way around the outside of the station with a train of flat wagons. The cattle siding appears to be in use for wagon storage and it is possible that the cattle dock was already out of use.
Photo: J. McCulloch

124. (Above) Grimsby, n.d. Mr. Alan Pegler, then the proud owner of the loco, can be seen leaning out of the cab of preserved Gresley Class A3 4-6-2 4472 *Flying Scotsman* as it crosses Wellowgate with a special in the late 1960's. With the exception of the BR Britannias, Pacific type locomotives were rare visitors to the area. *Flying Scotsman* appeared several times after preservation but otherwise the only recorded visits so far traced were in 1954 when Thompson Class A2 No. 60507 *Highland Chieftain*, on an empty stock train, and Peppercorn Class A1 No. 60128 *Bongrace*, to test the turntable at Cleethorpes, were noted, and on 12th June 1960 when Class A4 60022 *Mallard* hauled the Lincolnshire Poacher special from Grimsby to Edinburgh via Carlisle and the Waverley route.
Photo: D. Stockton

125. Grimsby Town, 23rd October 1964. WD Class 8F 2-8-0 90514 is crossing Wellowgate and entering platform 1 at Grimsby Town with a ballast train on 23rd October 1964. Note the loop lines going off to the left and the fact that the down loop actually forms a diamond crossover with the line out of platform 2 on Wellowgate crossing. *Photo: R. Ellis*

126. Grimsby Town, c.1959. The station pilot, Class A5 4-6-2T 69829, is seen taking refreshment from the water column at the west end of platform 2 at Grimsby Town. Standing on the tank top is shunter Denis Cooling and in the cab are Grimsby Town station inspector George Cumbidge and fireman Les Vivens. The driver was holding the camera.
Photo: R. Dane

127. Grimsby Town, c.1880. Grimsby Town station from Wellowgate circa 1880. Note the locomotive pit at the end of platform 2 and the leaning wall where platform 3 would eventually be built.

Photo: GCRS Collection

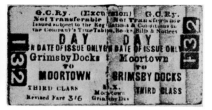

128. Grimsby Town, c.1910. Grimsby Town station from Wellowgate.

Photo: Grimsby Public Libraries

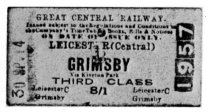

129. (Below) Grimsby Town, c.1898. Grimsby Town station staff in the closing years of the 19th century. Few names are now known but on the back row the last two on the right are Cotterill and Rushby and the portly gentleman with a white moustache and beard in the centre row, third from right, is William Charlesworth, station master, who at one time held a similar position at Grimsby Docks. On his right, fourth from left, is Hill.

Photo: Mrs J. Baker

24TH AUG 1924

50 YEARS ON RAILWAY.

Grimsby Stationmaster's Long Record of Service.

After 50 years' service on the railway, Mr. Tom Jervis, stationmaster at Grimsby Town, retired yesterday.

The son of a railwayman, and born at a cottage overlooking the station where eventually he became master, he entered the service of the old Manchester, Sheffield and Lincolnshire Railway Company as office boy at 5s. a week.

He was on night duty when the rioters delivered an attack on the company's property at Grimsby Docks, and he sent the telegram down the line to Sheffield which summoned military aid.

Mr. T. W. Jervis.

Transfers to New Holland and Brigg were followed by promotion to Sturton, and at 25 he became the youngest stationmaster in the service.

Later he became stationmaster at Barnby, Dunn, Silkstone and Mottram, and finally the ambition of a lifetime was achieved when he was appointed master at Grimsby Docks, where his railway career started as a junior clerk.

Courtesy – Mrs. J. Baker

131. Grimsby Town, 9th May 1962. The interior of Grimsby Town station looking east from the footbridge, a parcels train for Peterborough is standing in platform 2 whilst a four car DMU is entering platform 3 with a train from Cleethorpes. Since this photograph was taken offices have been built at the east end of platform 1 and the W. H. Smiths kiosk, along with a smaller one on platform 2, are now but a memory. *Photo: G. Biddle*

132. (Below) Grimsby Town, n.d. The Yarborough Hotel dominates almost every view taken of Grimsby Town station. It is visible here in the centre background as Class B1 4-6-0 No. 61190 pulls out of the station with the Cleethorpes portion of a train from Peterborough. It became the practice at Town station for down GC line trains, i.e. trains for Cleethorpes, to use platform 1, up GC line trains to use mainly platform 3 and occasionally platform 2, and GN line trains, whether up or down, to use platform 2. *Photo: J. McCulloch*

133. Grimsby-Holme Street, 21st May 1961.
The 7.30 am Daybrook – Cleethorpes excursion hauled by Class B1 4-6-0 No. 61166 about to cross Holme Street level crossing on 21st May 1961. The close proximity of the crossings at Pasture Street and Holme Street can be seen to good effect in this view with the front bogie of the engine already on Holme Street whilst the third coach of the train is astride Pasture Street. In the right background is Hewitts brewery which for many years kept the surrounding area supplied with beer. Unfortunately, like so many other small independent breweries, it was unable to survive the pressure from the larger companies and subsequently was taken over by Bass Charrington. No commercial beer is now brewed in the area and new law courts are now being built on the site.
Photo: J. Willerton

134. Grimsby-Holme Street, April 1961.
Class 9F 2-10-0 No. 92193 takes the junction onto the East Lincs line at Holme Street with a Saturday afternoon fish train for London. Originally double track, this arm of the Holme Street – Goods Junction – Garden Street triangle had been singled by this time and down trains gained the correct road at Holme Street via the crossover just behind the locomotive. The line on the extreme left was a relief line that ran from Garden Street to Newmarket Street. *Photo: B. Clark courtesy Grimsby Public Libraries*

135. Grimsby-Holme Street, c.1955. The Dock Tower has been like a homing beacon to returning Grimbarians for more than a century and is visible from many parts of the town. In this view it appears in the background as Class K3 2-6-0 No. 61866 approaches Holme Street with a London bound fish train in the mid 1950's. It is in the area towards the rear of the train that the often proposed central station would have been built.

Photo: J. McCulloch

136. Grimsby-Holles Street, c.1924. Several of J. G. Robinson's final design of 4-6-0, the 9Q, were built after the grouping and classified B7 by the LNER. All but the last two however, appeared bearing Great Central numbers. One of this final batch, which had reduced boiler mountings to bring them within the LNER standard loading gauge, is seen passing Holles Street goods yard with a Cleethorpes – Manchester express. The goods shed on the left was demolished several years ago.
Photo: H. L. Lowe courtesy GLRPS

137. Grimsby-Central Market Goods, n.d. Until the outbreak of World War I the railways were predominantly a male preserve. However, with so many men away serving their country it became necessary to employ women in many grades. In this view a group of women porters, in rather unsuitable attire, are pictured unloading a van of margarine at Central Market goods depot during the war years. In the background is the Newmarket Street ornamental footbridge referred to in the text. Until it was replaced by a plate girder bridge in the late 1950's this bridge gave many a young boy an excellent view of the activities around East Marsh and Holles Street goods yard and of Grimsby loco.
Photo: Grimsby Public Libraries

138. (Below) Grimsby-East Marsh, 7th April 1964. The London fish passing East Marsh behind Class 9F 2-10-0 No. 92178. Arguably one of the finest types of locomotive ever built these large freight engines almost made the London fish their own private property during the few years they were based at Immingham.
Photo: J. Willerton

(310)

GREAT CENTRAL RAILWAY.

Via **GODLEY.**

FISH WAY BILL.

From **GRIMSBY ROYAL DOCK** to _____ on the _____ Rly., by _____ Train _____ 192__

SENDER	CONSIGNEE	ADDRESS	Under 2 cwt.—"Parcels." Numbers only to be abstracted—not the Weight.						2 cwt. and upwards.—"Miscellaneous." Weight only to be abstracted—not the Numbers.					No. of Truck
			No. and Description of Packages	Weight cwt. qrs. lbs.	Paid on s. d.	TO PAY £ s. d.	Paid £ s. d.		No. and Description of Packages	Weight cwt. qrs. lbs.	Paid on s. d.	TO PAY £ s. d.	Paid £ s. d.	

139. Grimsby M.P.D., c.1930. Probably due to its demotion to sub shed upon the opening of Immingham it has been difficult to trace many views of Grimsby loco. On this page we show three of the handful we have found.

In this view a Class K3 2-6-0 is taking on water alongside New Bridge signal box with the coal stage, part of the running shed and the water softener visible in the background. The vantage point is Newmarket Street footbridge and the date circa 1930.
Photo: N. Camplejohn

140. Grimsby M.P.D., c.1935. Driver George Willerton alongside Class K3 2-6-0 167 shortly before working a fish train in the 1930's.
Photo: J. Willerton

141. Grimsby M.P.D., June 1955. A Saturday lunchtime at Grimsby loco in June 1955 and the pilots are returning to shed for servicing over the weekend. Three Class J94's and a Class J63 are visible in this view taken from the site of the turntable. At one time Grimsby had a requirement for 18 pilots, today it requires one.
Photo: J. Hewson

142. (Above) Grimsby Docks, 3rd April 1965. DMU's arrived early in the area and took over the majority of the local passenger turns. However, not all succumbed and right to the end of steam some turns regularly produced a steam locomotive. One such duty was the 5.57 pm Cleethorpes – Doncaster. Doncaster based Class B1 4-6-0 No. 61326 is seen at Grimsby Docks station with this train on 3rd April 1965, less than a year before the end of steam in the area.

Photo: J. Willerton

143. Grimsby Docks, 31st December 1955. Class J94 0-6-0ST No. 68033 is reversing through Grimsby Docks station on New Years Eve with a train of loaded coal wagons. The train is on the curve between Docks station and Union Dock swing bridge.

Photo: J. Willerton

LONDON & NORTH EASTERN RAILWAY.

DATE

From GRIMSBY DOCKS

TO .... (L.N.E. G.N. Section)

Via RETFORD and NEWARK

Consignee ....

Owner and No. of Wagon .... Total Sheets ....

144. Grimsby Docks. A further example of wartime female staff. These girls are posing for the camera at Grimsby Docks station.

Photo: Grimsby Public Libraries

POINT DUTY

145. (Above) Cleethorpe Road Level Crossing, c.1960. In the text we refer to the dire need over many years for a bridge or subway to avoid the delays caused by the railway at this point. This view, taken around 1960, shows the havoc caused by the passing of one train. Traffic can be seen tailing back beyond Riby Square whilst the queue on this side of the crossing would probably have extended as far as Lock Hill if not further. Note the dock workers gaining access to Cleethorpe Road before the gates are fully open and the traffic blocks the exit from the docks. To take this photograph today the photographer would have to stand in the middle of Cleethorpe Road flyover which opened as the rail traffic diminished in 1967. *Photo: Grimsby Evening Telegraph*

147. Grimsby Docks, 21st April 1966. The view is taken looking across Cleethorpe Road from the footbridge at Grimsby Docks station. The main line can be seen curving away to the right with the sidings for fish traffic fanning outwards towards the Grimsby Cold Store in the background. This building was originally a grain warehouse and, now that the cold store sign has been removed, once again proudly displays, in tiled letters, the legend Great Northern Railway. The view was taken just a few months before the fish trains were withdrawn. *Photo: H. B. Priestley*

Authors note:— Trains are controlled by signalmen and not by policemen.

148. Grimsby-Royal Dock, 30th April 1964. Fish trains were marshalled at two points. East Side, Royal Dock and New Clee. In this view Class B1 4-6-0 No. 61098 is on the curve from Fish Dock Road to Cleethorpe Road and is passing East Side with a fish train for Banbury from New Clee.
Photo: J. Willerton

L. N. E. R.
GRIMSBY DOCKS.
Pass the SAILING Vessel

0000

OUT OF FISH DOCK.
.............Tons (Gross Register) at 2d. per Ton.
Paid £.   s.   d.

149. Grimsby-Royal Dock, 8th April 1958. The East Side, Royal Dock was better known to railwaymen as New Dock. It is at New Dock that Class 4F 0-6-0 No. 44412 is seen waiting to back down onto the Nottingham fish on 8th April 1958. After nationalisation this train often produced ex LMS locomotives, usually Hughes-Fowler Class 5MT 2-6-0's or Stanier Class 5MT 4-6-0's, but it was not uncommon for 4F's to be allocated to this duty. It was also possible on occasions to see one of Nottingham's BR Standard Class 4MT 4-6-0's of the 75xxx series on this working.
Photo: J. Willerton

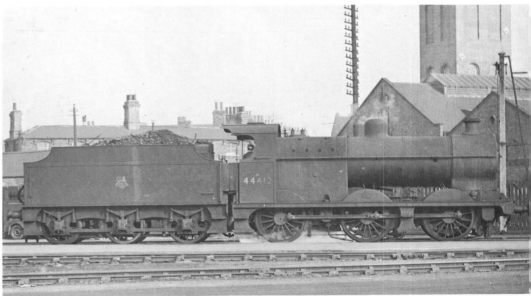

150. Grimsby-Royal Dock, c.1930. The East Side, Royal Dock, viewed from the north end of the yards. The tremendous amount of rail activity that was once such a vital part of the economy of Grimsby and employed so many locomotives on pilot work is so much in evidence that it is hard to believe that today there is not one rail in use on this side of the dock. The locomotive busily engaged in shunting wagons is an ex Hull & Barnsley Railway 0-6-0T (LNER Class J75).
Photo: H. L. Howe
courtesy Grimsby-Louth RPS

151. Grimsby-Union Dock, c.1930's.
This view of the swing bridge over the Union Dock was taken, looking north, in the 1930's. Above the bridge, and in the process of demolition, is the gantry which served the coal hoists in the Royal Dock before the construction of the underground conveyors referred to in the caption for the photograph on pages 48 and 49. West Bank sidings signal box is visible beyond the gantry. Note the number of LNER cast iron warning signs visible.
Photo: H. L. Howe courtesy GLRPS

152. Grimsby-Union Dock, c.1930's.
An alternative view of the demolition work on the coaling gantry, taken on the same day as the view above. With the removal of the gantry it was possible to remodel the track layout and renew the quayside along the Union Dock. Some of the work along the quay is visible in this view. Beyond the gantry a Class J50 can be seen on pilot duty whilst alongside wagons are filled by hopper. The signal box at centre right is Union Dock.
Photo: H. L. Howe courtesy GLRPS

153. (Below) Grimsby-Royal Dock, May 1955. Views of railway activity on the west side of the Royal Dock, the side that is still rail connected, are very few. However, Class J94 0-6-0ST No. 68026 was caught by the camera during a break in shunting duties in May 1955. On the right is Doigs shipyard where many of the trawlers which once sailed from the port were built or repaired. Like the deep sea trawling fleet Doigs shipyard is no more. *Photo: J. Hewson*

154. (Left) Grimsby-Murray Street, October 1954. The Cleethorpes line is beyond the concrete wall on the left of this view of Class J63 0-6-0T No. 68204 in Murray Street in October 1954. It is waiting to take a van across Fish Dock Road into the marshalling area at New Dock, visible in the centre background. Note the use of a flagman to warn traffic of the approach of the locomotive, a necessity in this area of the dock where there was not a reserved section for the railway. *Photo: J. Hewson*

157. (Right) Grimsby-Humber Street, 1960. The bridge at Humber Street frames Class K3 2-6-0 No. 61835 as it approaches New Clee station with an excursion for Cleethorpes in 1960. At one time there was a small mechanical coaling facility on the extreme right of this view. The houses on the left, like the buildings at the nearby station, are now but a memory whilst the only part of the railway to remain is the track on the left. Beneath the arches of the bridge which saw countless fish vans pass through on their way to and from the Pontoon over the years, there now runs a road serving the factories and cold stores which have replaced the sidings at this point. *Photo: P. Loftis*

155. (Left) Grimsby-Murray Street, June 1955. Class J63 0-6-0T No. 68207 is seen in June 1955 waiting to proceed along Murray Street to gather fish vans but its way is blocked by a lorry. The Pontoon is on the right whilst the Cleethorpes line runs at the back of the buildings on the left. *Photo: J. Hewson*

158. (Right) New Clee, c.1968. New Clee station could never be described as busy except on the occasions when excursions ran in connection with a football match at nearby Blundell Park, home of Grimsby Town F.C. Although the station has remained open the buildings have long since been demolished and, as can be seen, the signal box was closed when this view was taken in the late 1960's. *Photo: Lens of Sutton*

156. (Left-lower) Grimsby-Humber Street, c.1958. Class K3 2-6-0 No. 61956 slowly negotiates the curve at Humber Street with a fish train from New Clee in the late 1950's. It is at this point where the severe reverse curves, extending to Fish Dock Road, commence. Until the extension of No. 2 Fish Dock in 1894 the line carried straight on and would have disappeared out of view on the left instead of on the right. *Photo: J. McCulloch*

159. (Right) New Clee, n.d. A sight so common until the mid 1960's that few railway enthusiasts realised how soon it would all be swept away. On summer weekends excursions would roll into Cleethorpes almost nose to tail. A typical summer Sunday would see young trainspotters cycling along the Humber Bank in a morning to Immingham to try and get round the shed without being caught, a risky business which often resulted in being chased from the premises by an irate foreman. Then, home for lunch and in the afternoon another cycle ride up to Cleethorpes to see what had worked in on the days excursions before going home to tea and back to Wellowgate or one of the other level crossings in the town to watch these trains leave, in case one had been missed.

This is often the sight that would greet them at New Clee and Suggitts Lane in an afternoon and as each engine came into view the oft heard cry of "not another B1" could be heard. Would that we could visit New Clee or stand at Wellowgate and say that today. Taken at New Clee on an August Bank Holiday Monday in the late 1950's, nine excursions are lined up ready to return to Cleethorpes station and start their homeward journey. Left to right are three unidentified B1 4-6-0's, Class D11 4-4-0 No. 62668 *Jutland*, K3 2-6-0 No. 61824, B1 Nos. 61208 and 61231, K3 No. 61803 and D11 No. 62660 *Butler Henderson*. The only survivor is *Butler Henderson* which can be seen preserved and restored to its original GCR livery at Loughborough. *Photo: N. E. Stead*

160. Cleethorpes, c.1958. Class K3 2-6-0 No. 61950 is seen heading away from Cleethorpes at Fuller Street with a homeward bound excursion in the late 1950's whilst Class K2 2-6-0 No. 61728 waits to back down past Suggitts Lane with a similar train. Blundell Park football ground is just out of view on the right.

Photo: J. A. G. H. Coltas

161 & 162. Cleethorpes-date in text. Excursion traffic in the 1950's and 1960's was generally hauled by B1 4-6-0's, K2 and K3 2-6-0's and D11 4-4-0's although other ex LNER classes were used from time to time. These included V2 2-6-2's, B12, B16 and B17 4-6-0's, D16 and D49 4-4-0's and J11 and J39 0-6-0's. B.R. Standard types were also used, mainly Class 5MT 4-6-0's with an occasional Britannia Pacific appearing in the 1960's. From the LMS came the ubiquitous Class 5MT 4-6-0 and the Hughes-Fowler "Crab" Class 5MT 2-6-0's with, on occasions, Class 4F 0-6-0's, Class 8F 2-8-0's, Ivatt Class 4MT 2-6-0's, Jubilee Class 5XP 4-6-0's and on one memorable occasion a Stanier Class 5MT 2-6-0, the only recorded visit by such a locomotive to the area. There was also a Birmingham – Cleethorpes train which was rostered to an Immingham B1 but which produced ex LMS Class 4P Compound 4-4-0's on occasions circa 1954. All in all Cleethorpes saw a varied and interesting group of locomotives during this period and two of these are shown here at Suggitts Lane in the 1950's.

In the upper view "Crab" Class 5MT 2-6-0 No. 42823 is seen backing the Mansfield Holiday Express into Suggitts Lane sidings on 1st August 1955. In the lower view Class 8F 2-8-0 No. 48553 is setting out for home with a train load of tired but happy day trippers. Suggitts Lane signal box appears to be out of use but it stood so for many a year and was possibly only used on summer weekends when additional trains necessitated its attention.

Photo: J. Hewson and N. E. Stead respectively

163. Cleethorpes, 2nd October 1965. In 1965 the RCTS ran the North Lincolnshire Railtour hauled throughout by Britannia Class 7P 4-6-2 No. 70012 *John of Gaunt*. The locomotive is seen here being turned on Cleethorpes turntable prior to proceeding to New Holland and Barton. No 70012 also ventured onto New Holland Pier which was officially out of bounds to this type of loco, although during 1963 three of Immingham's allocation took football excursions onto the pier on the same day, before running its train to Barton tender first. At Barton, it was necessary to run round the train which it did just, there being only inches to spare on the passing loop. *Photo: C. J. Paine*

164. Cleethorpes, c.1930's. When this photograph was taken in the late 1930's Class D7 4-4-0 No. 5684 was one of only two survivors, both allocated to New Holland, of a class of locomotive that had been a familiar sight in the area since their introduction by the MS&LR in 1890. It is seen in platform 4 at Cleethorpes with a stopping train for New Holland.
Photo: GCRS

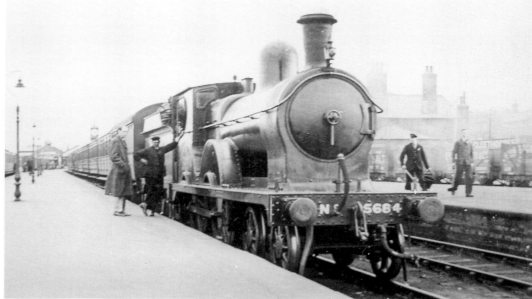

165. Cleethorpes, 9th May 1946. An evening train for New Holland is awaiting departure from platform 5 behind Class C4 4-4-2 No. 5358. With the exception of the short bay behind the photographer, platforms 5 and 6 were closest to the seashore and were often, as in this photograph, covered in sand blown off the beach. Above the tender of the loco is the clock tower which has welcomed visitors to Cleethorpes for many years.
Photo: H. C. Casserley

166. Cleethorpes, c.1930's. A fine line up of excursions awaiting departure from Cleethorpes in the 1930's. The locomotives are Class J2 0-6-0 No. 3079 in platform 5, Class J39 0-6-0's Nos. 2700 and 1269 in platforms 4 and 3 respectively and Class B6 4-6-0 No. 5416 in platform 2. Opposite the buffer stops at the end of platforms 3 and 4 is the No. 2 Refreshment Rooms where a tasty pint of beer can often be sampled. There is a story that on one occasion some people were partaking of this brew and idly watching a train backing down into either platform 3 or 4. They watched as the train came closer and closer and overrode the buffers and kept on coming. The idle watchers ran as the rear coach mounted the platform and came to rest jammed between the platform and the canopy. It is only a story but possibly true but if it did occur you can be sure that hardly a drop of their favourite tipple would have been lost.

Photo: Welholme Galleries

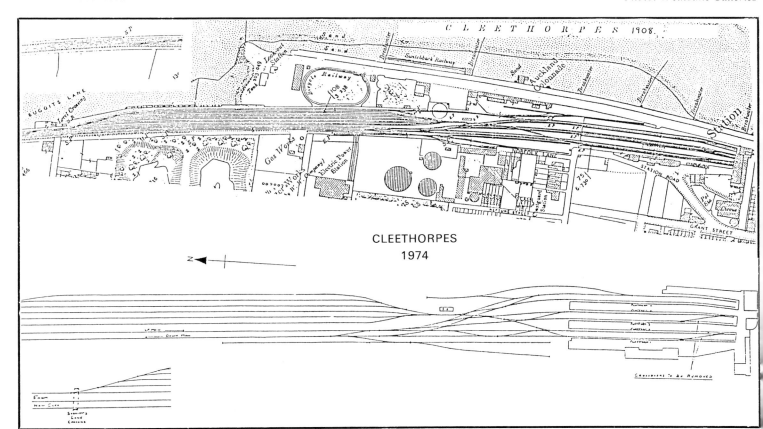

CLEETHORPES
1974

167. Grimsby, c.1921. Ivatt large boilered Atlantic (Class C1 4-4-2) No. 288 is rounding the curve between Garden Street and Goods Junction with a Peterborough bound semi-fast. The photograph dates from about 1921, evidenced by the GNR lettering on the tender of the locomotive, at which time these engines were the premier express type operating on the Great Northern.
Photo: H. L. Howe courtesy GLRPS

168. (Above) Grimsby, n.d. Typifying the afternoon passenger train departures from Grimsby is this view of Class B1 4-6-0 No. 61142 passing Goods Junction with a Peterborough train. A closer look at the rear of the train reveals a cluster of fish vans. This was a regular procedure with many passenger trains with the vans being attached either at Grimsby Town for East Lincs line trains or Grimsby Docks for GC line trains. Even DMU's were called upon to haul these vans. The entrance to the electricity works is on the left with the gas works on the right. *Photo: J. McCulloch*

169. Grimsby-Peakes Tunnel, 21st February 1955. To the majority of people a tunnel is long and dark and bored under a large hill or through a range of mountains. Peakes Tunnel, however, is nothing more than a brick overbridge carrying a farm track over the East Lincs line on the outskirts of Grimsby. WD Class 8F 2-8-0 No. 90085 has just passed through the "tunnel" on a wintry day in 1955. *Photo: J. McCulloch*

170. (Above) Grimsby-Peakes Tunnel, 11th July 1955. The low sunlight of a warm summers evening casts the shadow of Class B1 4-6-0 No. 61182 and its train on the cutting as it approaches Peakes Tunnel with a Peterborough – Grimsby train. The East Lincs line is typified in this view with the track stretching away into the distance in a straight line. Between Goods Junction and Louth there were only two noticeable curves, and these were not severe, south of Halton Village Halt and approaching Louth North. *Photo: J. McCulloch*

171. Waltham, c.1930's. The rural Station Road, New Waltham in the 1930's. The platforms of Waltham station are on either side of the road with the station house on the right and the signal box opposite.

Photo: Welholme Galleries

172. Waltham, 19th August 1961. Opened in 1848 as Waltham and Humberston, the latter name was eventually dropped and the station became known simply as Waltham. Of typical East Lincs line construction with staggered platforms and a station house, partly visible on the right, along the roadside. The arrival of the railway brought new construction and the area around the line is now a thriving village known, appropriately, as New Waltham.

Photo: D. Thompson

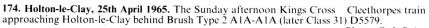
174. Holton-le-Clay, 25th April 1965. The Sunday afternoon Kings Cross — Cleethorpes train approaching Holton-le-Clay behind Brush Type 2 A1A-A1A (later Class 31) D5579.
Photo: C. J. Paine

175. Grainsby, 19th August 1961. Possibly one of the smallest stations inherited by British Railways in 1948 was the halt at Grainsby. Extremely difficult to find on a dark night it never really justified its existence and closed in 1952. In this view, the platforms are still neat and tidy almost ten years after closure. Note the water churns on the down platform which were for the gatehouse.
Photo: D. Thompson

173. Holton-le-Clay, n.d. This signal box was of standard East Lincs line pattern and stood alongside Holton-le-Clay station. This station was originally called Holton-le-Clay and Tetney and was, in fact, much closer to Tetney than Holton-le-Clay although the name was dropped many years ago.
Photo: R. Barnard

176. North Thoresby, c.1905. North Thoresby station was the only intermediate station between Grimsby and Louth to remain open until the withdrawal of passenger services in October 1970. This view, probably taken circa 1905, is looking north with a GNR 0-6-0 busily engaged on the daily pick up goods working and managing to block both running lines while it sorts out the wagons it requires.
Photo: Courtesy GLRPS

177. Ludborough, c.1900. This delightful photograph shows a farmer delivering milk churns for onward shipment to either Grimsby or Louth. Like so many other country stations Ludborough was not in the village of that name but about half way between it and Fulstow. *Wellholme Galleries*

178.Fotherby, 19th August 1961. The final station, or more correctly halt, before Louth, was at Fotherby, seen here looking north. The gatehouse, on the left, is of standard ELR design and compares with that at Utterby, There were similar structures at Grainsby, Holton Village and at Welsby Road in Grimsby. Note the steps on either platform which could be wheeled into place to assist passengers boarding or alighting from trains. *D Thompson*

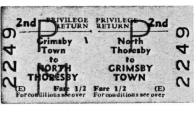

(Bottom-left) 179 & (Bottom-right) 180. Steam took a long time to return to the Grimsby area after the visits by the *Flying Scotsman* in the early 1970's, although numerous steam locomotives have made their way into and out of the country via Immingham Docks, albeit on the back of lorries. The return of live standard gauge steam came on 20th May 1995, F A Cup Final day, when Class 5MT 4-6-0 No **44767** *George Stephenson* worked into Cleethorpes the "The Humbersider" excursion. The logistical problems of turning the locomotive were possibly the the most interesting part of the visit as it gave enthusiasts four opportunities to record the locomotive at different points in the area.This was due to the fact that there were no turntables and the triangles at Garden Street and Marsh Junction were long gone. Arriving more than two hours late, the locomotive then ran light to Habrough where it turned on the Habrough-Brocklesby-Ulceby triangle before returning tender first to Cleethorpes. 44767 is seen here (right) running light alongside Marsden Road on the Fish Docks on its way out to Habrough to turn and (left) storming its way through Great Coates with the return train. *both: Paul King*